REBIRTHING

REBIRTHING
FREEDOM FROM YOUR PAST

DEIKE BEGG

North Atlantic Books
Berkeley, California

Published by
North Atlantic Books
P.O. Box 12327
Berkeley, California 94712

ISBN 1-55643-546-0
Library of Congress Catalog Card Number 2004024146

First published in Great Britain by Thorsons, 1999
Printed in the United States of America
Distributed to the book trade by Publishers Group West

Rebirthing: Freedom from Your Past is sponsored by the Society for the Study of Native Arts and Sciences, a nonprofit educational corporation whose goals are to develop an educational and crosscultural perspective linking various scientific, social, and artistic fields; to nurture a holistic view of arts, sciences, humanities, and healing; and to publish and distribute literature on the relationship of mind, body, and nature.

North Atlantic Books' publications are available through most bookstores. For further information, call 800-337-2665 or visit our website at www.northatlanticbooks.com.

Substantial discounts on bulk quantities are available to corporations, professional associations, and other organizations. For details and discount information, contact our special sales department.

---

1 2 3 4 5 6 7 8 9 DATA 09 08 07 06 05 04

This book is dedicated to my teachers, who gave so generously and selflessly of themselves and their time, and to all my clients, who, for a brief period, courageously entrusted me with the care of their souls.

 CONTENTS

 # FOREWORD

According to the ancient Hindu prophecies recorded in the Puranas we are now living in a time of great turmoil and spiritual upheaval. We are, these prophecies say, in the final phase of the Age of Kali, the last of four enormous periods of time when all the 'impure residues' of thousands of years of human folly and negative karma will erupt into our psyches, our bodies and our societies, creating strange illnesses and psychological disturbances of every kind, as well as huge social degeneration.

But these prophecies also hint that as the Kali Age accelerates towards its ineluctable climax, teachings, hidden doctrines and extraordinary healing techniques will also arise to enable us to cleanse these residues. For the Kali Age is also a time of great purification – the Hopi Indians have a similar view – when, in the words of St John's Apocalypse 'the former things are passed away.'

The techniques of Rebirthing and recalling past lives were naturally known to ancient yogis and shamans the world over, but they were not widely taught to most people. Today we are once more being given these powerful tools and regaining a fuller understanding of the human psyche and its higher states of consciousness so that we can purify the agonies of our unfortunate birth circumstances past and present, and release the traumatic residues of abandonment, violence and premature deaths from past lives. This is a time, as Stanislav Grof has put it, of grand 'spiritual emergence.'

All such residues are imprinted in the subtle body or energy field that 'descends' into matter at conception to 'program' our present karma at every level down to the cellular. These karmic patternings become the unconscious psycho-spiritual blueprints for our lives and determine our psychological development, our health patterns and our fate in general. Heavy accumulation of unreleased or unresolved karmic patterns leads, when not made conscious, to difficult births, tragic life stories, addictions, disease and 'all the heartache and the thousand natural shocks that flesh is heir to.'

Since birth and death are the two poles of the great cycle of re-birth it is only natural, as Deike Begg shows us so clearly and compassionately, that Rebirthing and Past Life Therapy are essential complements to each other. In the early days of the Rebirthing movement, when I did my own training in America, past life memories tended to be pushed aside – mostly, I suspect, out of ignorance and fear. But now, thanks to Deike and to the work of Stanislav Grof, Chris Bache, Joy Manne and others, their fundamental complementarity is starting to be fully understood, giving us, in Deike's words 'a powerful therapeutic mix, if not *the* most powerful.'

Moreover, this felicitous mix is also a coming together of spirit and matter. For as this book repeatedly reminds us, breath is spirit, is *pneuma* (Greek), is *prana* (Sanskrit); the Divine Wind 'that bloweth where it listeth.' Our own personal breath/spirit is our connection to the universal breath/spirit or Holy Spirit, so that to invite the divine breath into our deepest selves is to become 'inspired' by the highest power of all. No-one says it better than the great mystic Hildegard of Bingen, who was also a healer:

Holy Spirit
giving life to all life,
moving all creatures,
root of all things,
washing them clean,
wiping out their mistakes,
healing their wounds,
you are our true life,
luminous, wonderful,
awakening the heart
from its ancient sleep.

Roger J. Woolger Ph.D
Author of *Other Lives, Other Selves*
and *Healing Your Past Lives*

ACKNOWLEDGMENTS

For his unstinting encouragement, his love and patience and continuous willingness to support and inspire, I thank my husband, Ean.

My deepest appreciation and thanks to:

My editor, Elizabeth Hutchins, who so wisely and creatively made me aware of intuitive leaps and kept pulling me back to address hard facts. You made me think about things that I took for granted.

Michelle Pilley, my commissioning editor, who supported my vision patiently throughout the writing of this book.

Eileen Campbell, for your enthusiasm, honesty, support and, above all, your friendship.

Diana Roberts, my Rebirthing teacher, who warmly embraced me from the start and gave me my first opportunity to teach Rebirthing in a group.

Viki McKenzie, my Rebirther, who always knew exactly what I needed and who with her wisdom, love and compassion made my own Rebirth possible.

Del Palmer, my assistant at workshops, who so selflessly gives of his time, energy and expertise, and who intuitively knows what other people need.

Euan Laird, Consultant Obstetrician at the Horton Hospital in Banbury, Oxfordshire, who also so generously gave of his time and expertise to explain to me some of the medical complexities of childbirth.

Roger Woolger, for his unique and inspiring teaching, for his warmth and encouragement.

And my gratitude for their tremendous contribution to this book:

Oonagh Blackman, to whom I was a total stranger at first, for trusting me; Connie Burchell for profoundly enriching my life and opening my heart; Jane Carr for her courage to dare and 'breathe'; Joanna Davies-Evitt for her love and sensitivity; Alan Dillon for his determination to go on when no path seemed to lie ahead; Bonnie Greer for introducing me to the immense storehouse of creativity that rests in the breath; Lucy Howells for her courage to change; Francine Levinson for her child-like enthusiasm, strength and vulnerability, and for her determination to free herself from her past; Victoria Mosley for her fun, generosity, persistence and capacity to entertain; Helen McNerney, who courageously plunged into the unknown, trusting; Robin Parker for his friendship and inspiration; Senta Rich for filling my life with sunshine; Andrew Rich for challenging and forcing me to look deep into my own soul; Anri Schroff for her encouragement and enthusiasm and last but not least, Dawn and Giles Tilley for sharing themselves and their homes so generously with Ean and me.

I also wish to thank the many clients, colleagues and friends who wrote and telephoned and enquired how this book was progressing. Their contributions and heartfelt support throughout the writing process has been immense. Thank you also Louise Macdonnell, your informative and encouraging faxes always arrived just at the right moment.

PART 1 REBIRTH

1 A REBIRTHER IS BORN

Without an escort you are bewildered on a familiar road;
don't travel alone on a way you haven't seen at all;
don't turn your head away from the Guide.
Rumi

I had not seen Sally for a couple of years when we had lunch to discuss a ski trip I was organizing for a group of about twenty people. She had changed. She used to be a twitchy, agitated and fast-talking woman. The Sally who sat opposite me now was quiet, serene and composed. When I asked what had happened to bring about such a radical change, her face lit up and she explained that she had had three Rebirthing therapy sessions. 'It calms you down inside, aligns your energy centers and changes your life – all without trying too hard. You only need a few sessions.'

I had heard of so called 'quick fix' techniques and knew that there was no such thing. Yet here was Sally, claiming to have been transformed by a few hours of therapy. Good manners prevented me from expressing my doubts, but surely there must be some other explanation. After all, I had trained for more than five years as a psychotherapist and had received more than twice as many years of various types of therapy myself, including four years of Jungian analysis. I knew that far more than 'a few sessions' were needed to change a person's character and deal with complexes, the dark side of the psyche and so forth. Psychotherapy is a complex business and can take years. How could a few sessions of Rebirthing therapy possibly change one's life?

'I can't wait to get away to the mountains,' Sally went on, smiling. 'I have taken up watercolor painting recently and will take my paints with me. I started painting after my second Rebirthing session. Always had wanted to, but never felt motivated enough.' She placed a photograph of a landscape watercolor on the table. I was impressed. Sally had never shown artistic talent of any kind before.

At this point I had no intention of having anything to do with Rebirthing myself. I didn't understand exactly what Sally meant by it anyway. I had vaguely heard about it but regarded it as 'fringe' – something that attracts those people who want their lives to change for the better but only if it essentially means no change on their part and no effort. When Sally offered the name and telephone number of her Rebirther I wrote them down out of politeness, but I had no real interest in what I regarded as a transient gimmick.

Sally explained that during Rebirthing, people often re-experience their birth and even life inside the womb, that they see all kinds of images and have strange sensations. But none of it made any sense to me. I knew nothing that I could compare it with and I told her so. 'You've got to experience it for yourself,' she said. 'It's like trying to explain to someone the taste of strawberries when they have never seen or tasted any. It takes all your fears away,' she continued, 'and it cured the stiffness in my neck and shoulders that no amount of massage could relieve permanently.'

I was still not convinced. Rebirthing! The word itself did not make me feel comfortable. It conjured up images of a black abyss, hellfire and horror, bringing back a recurring nightmare I had had all through my childhood and from which I always awoke screaming. No, this was not for me. Give me the talking therapy any time. That at least is a sound and sure way of uncovering past traumas and dealing with them safely. Little did I know that I would pick up the phone one day and book a Rebirthing session that would change my life within a surprisingly short period of time.

A year later I had reached a critical turning point. I had just broken off with a man I loved deeply but who was not free. I saw no future in continuing a relationship with someone who was never available at weekends and I didn't feel that I had the moral right to demand changes. It was the most difficult decision I had ever made. We had been very close for almost five years, but I felt now the time had come to free myself and get on with my life. My own marriage had broken down and I had been left with three teenage children to support. I felt deeply unhappy, stuck, frightened and abandoned by everyone, including God. I needed to take stock. I began to ask myself serious questions about what I was doing and what I was doing it for. Until now I had always been able to find a way out of difficulties. After all, that was my job as a psychotherapist. Yet here I was, forty years old, with no personal future that I could envisage.

I had also made a name for myself as an astrologer. I was regularly travelling to various parts of the world, lecturing, giving workshops and being consulted by an endless stream of clients. The phone never seemed to stop ringing and I had started to feel that my life no longer belonged to me. My children were going through crucial educational phases and needed me there to talk to and encourage them. Everyone else's need seemed greater than mine. I was highly regarded in my professions but my private life was a mess. How could it all have gone so wrong?

Looking back, it wasn't all that wrong, but at the time I felt that I would never be happy again and that I would never find a man who would actually be there for me, support and comfort me, someone I could share my life with.

At the same time, though, paradoxically, I could not believe that this is how my life would be from now on. At some level I knew that life was not meant to be like this. There must be something more than working and earning money. I knew deep down inside that something had to happen. I could not continue living in this way, for I no longer saw the point. I had lost sight of what my needs were. I had forgotten that I had any.

One wet day I sat watching the raindrops chasing one another down the window pane and I thought of Sally and the fun we had had chasing each other down the ski slopes the previous year. She did do some painting, but most of all we had a lot of fun. Sally's exuberance, generosity and huge amounts of energy had made her the most popular member of the group and her skiing came on in leaps and bounds too. I smiled to myself, for the first time in over a week, as I looked for, and finally found, the piece of paper with the Rebirther's phone number.

Her name was Annette and she worked from a large old house in south London. The room was huge, cold and empty except for a settee and a mattress in the middle of the floor. I was feeling nervous. The building was used as a centre for all types of therapies and I could hear loud voices, music and strange slapping noises in the background. My God, I thought, what have I let myself in for?

Annette smiled at me and gently asked me a few questions about myself and why I had come. Then she asked me to take a card from a pack. 'Ah, Maya, the great spinner in the sky,' she whispered mysteriously. 'This is the card of fate and your picking this card shows that you are under the influence of fate, that your life is already mapped out and that you have nothing to fear.'

Oh yeah, I thought to myself, nothing to fear? My relationship has just died, I have three permanently hungry mouths to feed and I am miserable as hell. What would she know about that?

Annette must have picked up my doubts, because she went on to say: 'You have a job to do in this life. You have come here to teach and everything that you are going through at the moment is part of a learning phase. This is a time of necessary conflict. Harmony will follow.' Well, I couldn't argue with that. How did I know what the future would hold for me? I felt so vulnerable that I was ready to believe anything. All I knew for certain at that moment was that I was lonely, unhappy, depressed and feeling hopeless.

Annette placed a white candle next to the mattress and lit it. Then she asked me to lie down under the blanket and sat down at some distance from me on the floor. She explained how she wanted me to breathe and that I would be breathing for approximately one hour. At first it was easy, but soon the effort of maintaining the rhythm and intensity began to tire me. But at least whilst I was concentrating on breathing I wasn't thinking and that in itself was a relief.

Annette had given me no other instruction but to breathe, and she neither uttered a word nor touched me. I began to feel lonely and abandoned and increasingly frustrated in keeping the breathing going. My skepticism was once again aroused. What a joke, I thought. What a way to make a living. I was angry with myself for having let myself in for this and just wanted to get out. After a while I became vaguely aware that I was angrily banging my arms and fists on the mattress.

By now I was in an altered state of consciousness, for although I was aware of my body movements and my frustration there was nothing I could do except keep breathing and bang my fists. I felt I had no ability whatsoever to influence the situation and just kept thinking that I wanted to get out of there. I also felt a sense of urgency and anger at the slowness of things. 'Damn it, come on!' I commanded myself again and again. 'Keep going!' I had absolutely no idea what I was doing or what was happening to me, but I was very angry and aware that something was 'blocking' me. I had the sense of having to get to somewhere on the 'other side.'

Then I heard a strange noise in my head, like water running through a pipe. This went on for a couple of minutes or so. Next I saw flashing lights and heard loud sounds like metal falling on metal. I saw people in white coats and masks and I knew in that instant that I was in an operating theatre and that I had just been born.

'Is it over?' I whispered.

'No,' said Annette, 'I don't think so. Oh, maybe it is.'

I didn't know what had happened. One minute I had been thrashing about on the mattress and the next I felt that I had just been born.

Then I felt the strangest sensation. A gentle stream of energy was slowly snaking its way up my body from my feet, gradually warming every part. A feeling of lightness, calm and utter security spread through me. My body felt totally integrated, with every part exactly in its right place, and although I also felt dazed and disoriented I felt highly charged with energy and strangely clear and lucid at the same time.

Everything will be alright, I heard myself thinking. It sounds crazy now but at that moment I felt tremendous love for Annette (who had been distant and detached throughout) and for the whole world. All Annette said was, 'You tried hard to be born. Your mother did not help you much but then somehow you were pushed out anyway. You stopped breathing for a few minutes. That is when you were born.'

I was too perplexed to ask any questions, but I *knew* that I had just experienced my birth and that I felt different. Something had gone from me, freeing me. I could not explain this to myself or anyone else then, but I was aware of a profound shift. A big burden had been lifted from me. All my worries were gone and my body felt cleansed and open, without a single point of tension – a condition I had never been able to induce so totally before with either yoga or meditation. I lay in this glow for a while before, reluctantly, getting up to leave. I made another appointment for the following week.

Driving home, still slightly confused and feeling not quite myself, the weirdest thing happened. It seemed as if a voice from above was saying to me, 'Hand your little will over to God!' Its clarity and loudness hit me like a lightning bolt and I had to pull over and stop the car. I don't know how long I sat there, stunned. The command seemed so strong and urgent that I simply said out loud, 'OK. From now on I will hand my will over to the universe. I will allow myself to be guided.'

This decision felt unshakable and in an instant I knew that I would leave all relationship matters up to fate, that I would trust that I and my children would be taken care of and that I needed to concentrate on my life's work. Until then I had always assumed responsibility for all decision-making, both for the children and for how my relationships should or would turn out. If one thing did not work I would try another. 'Where there is a will there is a way' was my motto. But now all my attempts to resolve my difficulties had only created more confusion and unhappiness. I had always felt that *I* was doing something wrong, that *I* could change other people's behavior towards me if only *I* would change. In that very moment I realized that I had always in some obscure way felt guilty about something, felt that I had never quite done enough of whatever I was meant to be doing. Then I felt a 'click' deep inside myself and a new attitude was born. I decided then and there to *let* things happen rather than *make* them happen. Never before had I experienced this kind of trust in a higher power, but at that moment I knew that all would be well.

I never did have that second session with Annette, although I did turn up for it. She thought I did not need it. The following week she emigrated to America to start a career as a psychic counselor.

That seemed to be the end of that, as far as I was concerned. I did not ask Annette to recommend anyone else nor did I know where to find another Rebirther. But I knew that I had stumbled on a most extraordinary therapy, even if for the time being I did nothing more about it. Christmas was approaching, the children were home for the holidays and I was organizing yet another skiing party. Three-and-a-half months later my life had completely changed.

For our skiing holiday we had chosen a small pretty village very high up in the Alps on the border between Italy and Austria. It was bitterly cold and a freezing blizzard added to the discomfort. On the first morning we assembled outside the ski instructors' hut to give a demonstration of our abilities so that they could group us accordingly. Underneath our skis we could feel the sheet ice; in fact, the ground we were standing on was like a skating rink. I have always hated skiing on ice and that morning I was nervous and not looking forward in the least to going up the drag lift.

When it was my turn to demonstrate my skills I tried to be confident and boldly did my little turn. What happened next was to change the course of my life forever. My skis slid on the ice and crossed over. I fell forward and in order to stop my face from hitting the frozen ground I threw out my left arm. I felt a sharp pain in my shoulder and once back on my feet I found I couldn't lift my left arm. I had lost all power in it.

I was taken to hospital and the X-rays revealed that I had broken my left shoulder. My whole upper body was put in plaster, leaving my right arm free and my left hand sticking out of the plaster in the middle of my chest.

When I returned to the hotel at lunchtime it was deserted, for everybody was still on the slopes, and the heating had been turned off. I was beginning to feel the shock of the injury and started feeling lonely and miserable. There was only one person I wanted to talk to for comfort at that moment and that was the man with whom I had broken off a month before. I had had no intention of ever contacting him again, but as if in a trance I dialled his number in London. He answered almost immediately. He was overjoyed to hear from me and we were both very emotional. He was extremely sympathetic, being an avid skier himself, and before we finished talking we agreed to meet the day after I returned. The relief, much to my surprise, was tremendous. I had no idea how much I had missed him. Now my mood lightened and I looked forward to a really good rest for the remainder of the holiday. Having one of my hands restricted meant that I needed help with some things like washing my hair and cutting up my food. I was forced to allow other people to look after me and as there was nothing I could do about it I sat back and enjoyed the attention.

Back in London we met as arranged and picked up our relationship where we had left it. I had decided not to control things any more, but rather let fate decide. Two days later, on January 1, his wife decided, for various reasons – one of them being that she had fallen in love with someone else – to leave him. It all happened so fast from then on that we had hardly time to catch our breath. Within a few days we were house-hunting and three months later he was divorced (I had already divorced a year earlier). It felt as though I no longer needed to do anything at all – life itself had assumed the direction I was to take from now on.

Eventually we did find a new home – not a house or a flat, but a houseboat on the Thames in Chelsea. This fact is significant because a few boats down from us was the *Colne Denton*, a large vessel on which a Rebirther training school had its headquarters. Its then owner, Viki MacKenzie, herself a trained Rebirther, became my Rebirther for the next few weeks. I booked ten sessions with her whilst at the same time starting the Rebirther training, which took about nine months to complete. Once I had qualified I started with great vigour and enthusiasm to Rebirth people, sometimes as many as four per day, certainly never less than ten per week. I soon started teaching for the school I had trained with and also giving my own workshops on our boat and later on the 'training ship.'

It was a very busy time. The pace only slowed because Ean and I started writing a guide book about all the European sites associated with the magician Merlin and needed to keep evenings and weekends free for this as well as spending time travelling. Then, the year after the book was published, we were married. It all just happened as if of its own accord. Neither of us had intended to ever get married again but fate had other plans. One day out of the blue he proposed and I accepted.

My story is not unusual for people who have had Rebirthing therapy. When undergoing this process life often changes effortlessly. You do not have to *do* anything to make these changes happen – except to go with the flow, stay in the present and not 'push the river.' As Rebirthing removes the blockages that stand in the way of who you are meant to be, the free flow of the life force within speeds you onward.

WHAT IS REBIRTHING?

For unless a man is born again as a child he cannot enter the kingdom of heaven.

What is Rebirthing? For me it is about rebirth of the soul. In Rebirthing you are taught how to consciously connect to your soul by connecting with spiritual energy and drawing it inside yourself with the breath. The effects of this are immediate and permanent. Every little step of progress is irreversible and every little step is an initiation for the soul. Essentially, Rebirthing is a breathing therapy in which you consciously connect to the divine power of the universe so that it will cleanse and transform you. It is *not* first and foremost concerned with the birth process and reliving the birth trauma. There are many people who have never experienced a rebirth in that sense during their sessions.

The Rebirthing process itself is based on a very specific advanced breathing technique. Developed in the early 1970s, mainly by the American Leonard Orr, it can have the most amazing results – physically, emotionally, mentally and spiritually.

Although it is safe to practice and powerfully life-enhancing, you should not, however, attempt to do it on your own at first. The changes that could occur during a session – variations in body temperature and strange feelings and vision for instance – need to be facilitated by a trained practitioner in order to provide you with the fullest benefit and lead you through to the final high point when you can experience your own bliss, inner light and union with a greater whole.

There are many misconceptions concerning Rebirthing. Some forms of breathing therapy using the conscious, connected Rebirthing breath are called not Rebirthing but breath work, breathing therapy or vivation, to name but a few. The technique is the same, but the approach is different. On the other hand, some breathing techniques that differ from Rebirthing also call themselves by that name, although their methods, aims and results are not the same. They do not employ conscious connected breathing in the same way and the aim is relaxation of the body and an increase in energy and well-being. It is important, therefore, that I point out what the form of Rebirthing that I practice is *not*.

It is not a breathing technique that consists of hyperventilation, i.e. where the emphasis is on rapid breathing which frequently results in forcing the exhale. It is not primarily a method of relaxation, although relaxation ensues quite naturally at the end of a session. It is not *only* paying attention to the breath and none to the thoughts that arise, although sometimes this is necessary. It is not a quick fix, although it is the fastest working therapy I know. And it is not something that you can learn over a few weekends.

HOW I DEVELOPED MY REBIRTHING WORK

The work I do developed out of my rich psychotherapeutic training background, with a sound grounding in Psychosynthesis, Jungian psychology, Gestalt therapy, with its emphasis on voice dialogue, past-life therapy and astrology. For seventeen out of the past twenty-six years I have undergone various types of psychotherapy myself. They were an adventurous journey and a wonderful opportunity for self-discovery. (Psychotherapy is not to be confused with psychiatric treatment, which often – and sometimes only – employs the use of drugs.)

My main professional training as a psychotherapist took place in London with the Psychosynthesis and Education Trust and my principal teachers were Diana Whitmore, one of its founders, Piero Ferucci (Roberto Assagioli's successor) and Judith Firman. Psychosynthesis, as the name suggests, is concerned with synthesizing all the various parts of a person into one unified psychic whole. Whatever method proves useful and effective in the search for greater psychic integration – such as bodywork, art therapy, sand play, dancing, movement, etc. – can be made use of. In fact, there is no limit to the type of therapeutic method that can be included in psychosynthetic work as long as it is good for the client and it *works*.

There were two techniques in particular, though, that appealed to me more than any of the others. One was the use of guided imagery and the other was Gestalt therapy. In guided imagery a person is taken on an inner journey, for instance up to a mountain top where they might meet their Higher Self in the form of a wise being, or they might descend into a cave deep within the bowels of the Earth to encounter a lost and perhaps long-forgotten fragment of themselves. The therapist guides the journey but does not interfere with any of the material that emerges for the client. The therapist will suggest, however, that the client stays with an image, even a frightening one, until it changes of its own accord into its non-distorted, essential quality. For instance a ferocious wolf encountered in a perilous forest may change, after confrontation and dialogue, into a psychopomp, a wise guide and teacher that leads a person more deeply into their own unconscious regions.

If on an inner journey someone gets stuck, let's say in a ravine or in a narrow tunnel, they are encouraged to stay with it and explore fully what it feels like and what deep thoughts and bodily sensations it might evoke. If they are afraid, the therapist will encourage them to stay with the fear until the feeling changes naturally.

Guided imagery, properly used, effectively employs the imagination to access memory buried deep within the tissue structure as well as in the brain memory. But on its own, without the use of conscious connected breathing, it cannot bring about the physical cleansing process of the cells and the brilliant and supernatural visionary experiences encountered in Rebirthing practice.

Gestalt therapy also uses the body as a sounding board and as a link to hidden fragments of ourselves, but here the eyes are generally kept open and one experiences oneself as one is in the very moment of therapy – it is a 'here and now therapy.' Much attention is given to body language, quality and tone of voice, tightness of muscles, etc., and the client is encouraged to go along with the fantasy they are having in the here and now.

For instance if you have an issue with your mother, father or partner but you feel that it is pointless to discuss it or you are afraid to do so, the Gestalt therapist can encourage you to act this out in therapy. You imagine that the other person is sitting in a chair opposite you and here and now you tell them how you feel about them. When you have done that you switch chairs and now become the other person and talk back as the one you feel oppressed, judged, unsupported or bullied by. This dialogue can go on for some time until some integration has taken place.

The philosophy behind this is that everything we see happening 'out there' is a projection of our own inner images, feelings, desires and thoughts. Gestalt therapy helps us to own what we project (from Latin *projicio ject*, 'throw forth') onto others. During a typical session bodily feelings are fully explored, for there is never a bodily sensation without a feeling and never a feeling that does not also manifest physically. The insights thus gained, and the owning of characteristics previously seen only in another person, lead to a deeper understanding of one's own *shadow* side (that part of oneself that one does not acknowledge, feels inferior about or is ashamed of and, therefore, projects) and to a more complete sense of who we are in essence. (A more detailed explanation of the meaning of projection is given on pages 163–8.)

The type of Rebirthing I practice rests on the shoulders, primarily, of these two types of therapy. Both are ideally suited for use in breathing work. Without their deeper dimensions breathing therapy can be shallow, meaningless and dull.

It is also important, if one wants to work in this meaningful way with the breath, to have an understanding of other cultures, of mythology, fairy tales and astrology. The imagery that can emerge during sessions is often of an archetypal (collective) nature, belonging to ancestral or racial memory and frequently of cosmic dimensions. It is a region diametrically opposed to our ordinary conscious world, a region that is inhabited by strange beings, shapes, colors and lights. It is useful for the Rebirthing therapist therefore to know that a snake is a symbol of wisdom, as well as a frightening image for some; that a spider, as Maya, is also the great celestial spinner of illusion and fate, even for those with a spider phobia.

During Rebirthing people frequently see images of the various planets, stars and constellations, and knowledge of astrology can be invaluable. The birth chart not only tells me much about a person's character, but also reveals the current cosmic conditions with which they need to co-operate. It can tell me whether a person is about to have a nervous breakdown or a spiritual emergence. It is interesting how many people come to Rebirthing when their birth charts are 'activated' by one of the outer planets: Uranus (sudden, unexpected changes), Neptune (dissolution of former way of being, sacrifice and renunciation) or Pluto (death and rebirth and empowerment). Certain planetary conditions promote a rapid Rebirth, others, such as Saturn, planet of limitation, embodying the informing principle, indicate that a major blockage to the flow of spiritual energy to and from the soul exists and needs to be dealt with and dissolved. This may take two or more sessions.

The bodywork of Gestalt therapy has proved immensely helpful when working with bodily symptoms during breathing sessions, whilst guided imagery not only makes it a joy to work with people's emerging stories but also enables me to guide them more deeply into their inner worlds. And my work with Subpersonalities (different aspects of ourselves that co-exist within us), which is also an important part of Psychosynthesis, greatly facilitates the process when different parts of the same person emerge during breathing sessions.

I have always 'known,' since very young, that whatever I was going through, whatever I was learning – languages, psychology, astrology, mythology, drawing, meditation, yoga, cooking, skiing, etc. – was for some purpose that would reveal itself one day. I have found this purpose in my work as a Rebirther. My form of Rebirthing comprises all that I am, all I know and all that I have experienced in this life and others. I myself am the tool that I use for efficient facilitation in Rebirthing work.

YOUR JOURNEY

With Rebirthing breathing you enter totally new territory, a *terra incognita*. You find yourself in the strangest lands and circumstances. Whilst you will not lose your connection with the world you live in here and now, at the same time you can have experiences of another world, a different dimension and time. The 'trick' in Rebirthing is to allow yourself to dwell in that unknown world for long enough for a transformation to occur. That world lies in what Deepak Chopra in his book *Quantum Healing* calls a 'gap.' In this gap creativity, inspiration, super-intelligence and supernatural visions have their abode.

You would not set out on a journey through unknown terrain without a map or a guide. It would be foolish to start out on your own without someone who knows what lies ahead, knows the road and knows how (but not where) it ends. The same applies to Rebirthing. The breathing, if done correctly, cannot do you any harm, but if you start off doing it on your own it could put you off. The most likely thing to happen would be that you would fall asleep, which would make the whole exercise pointless. It is the *consciousness* that we bring to rhythmic connected breathing that is the determining factor. Also, during the first few sessions you may need a great deal of encouragement just to keep breathing, and if you don't breathe nothing will happen. After several years of Rebirthing, I still prefer to do my breathing with someone else present, if only to keep me breathing rather than dropping off to sleep.

Although the Rebirthing breath is only a relatively simple technique, what we inhale with the breath is far more than just air. The air contains spiritual energy, *prana* or life force – the very stuff that makes manifestation in physical form possible. Breathing is our major source of, and main connection to, this empowering life energy which Robert Fludd called 'the super-celestial, invisible force that enters the body through the breath.'

During a Rebirthing session you have the unique opportunity to connect with this force far more strongly and consciously than during ordinary everyday awareness, inhaling many times the normal amount of energy. This power, to which each and every one of us has access, can bring about radical, even total, change. It is of such immensity that it can literally blast through any blockage in your body-mind that stands in its way. This may be a rigid mental attitude, a blockage in the intestines, a depression caused by the death of a loved one or an unwillingness to forgive someone. It may be a set of behavior patterns which you were taught when very young but which no longer serve your purpose. It may be your psychological conditioning regarding relationships or your attitude to sex, money and security.

The only qualification you need to make contact with this force is a willingness to do the breathing for a certain length of time (ranging from half an hour to one-and-a-half hours and on rare occasions even longer) and a trust in the transformative powers of the breath.

The Buddha taught that conscious observation of inhalation and exhalation leads eventually to the knowledge of liberation. When we breathe consciously we become aware of that which is normally unconscious. If we change the rhythm of our breathing we change our minds and the way to change the rhythm is to give attention to breathing. When giving attention to breathing and rhythm we transform air into magical essence.

In order to get the best out of a breathing session you will need to suspend your disbelief in a force greater than yourself. You will need to remain open to the incoming breath, keep breathing calmly and 'wait upon the will of heaven.' If you breathe, relax and allow things to happen, rather than trying to control them, you will have a Rebirth. You will come to a natural end of the breathing cycle when you either open your eyes spontaneously or drift into a gentle sleep, but before that you will have had one of the most astonishing experiences ever.

Sometimes the most amazing images of brilliant colors and patterns appear before your inner vision. Sometimes there is a very bright light, so bright that it ought to hurt your eyes but doesn't. Sometimes your whole body can feel as if it has become infused with this light, causing you to lose all sense of normal bodily awareness. (You have probably heard and read much about the divine light. Well, this is the only way I have ever been able to 'be in the light' and to have the light enter me.) Sometimes a numinous figure, a wise or even Christ-like being appears. Huxley, in *The Doors of Perception*, mentions reports of people who have had similar experiences through the use of hallucinogenic drugs:

> *Sometimes people see visions, which may be of Christ Himself.*
> *Sometimes they hear the voice of the Great Spirit. Sometimes they*
> *become aware of the presence of God and of those personal*
> *shortcomings which must be corrected if they are to do His will.*

Here are two examples from my own practice. Once, when on holiday in Majorca, I was asked by a German woman called Ute, who lives there, to give her a Rebirth. She was skeptical but wanted to try it with the view of organizing a workshop for me on the island. She needed a lot of encouragement to keep her breathing going for long enough for something to happen. But finally she broke through her own resistance and felt that she was in the presence of Jesus Christ, who was showing her his heart. She was so astonished that she kept crying out: 'This can't be true! What am I seeing?' Eventually, realizing that she was in the presence of something quite extraordinary, she succumbed to the experience and was so moved that when the session was over she asked me to leave as she wanted to go back inside herself and reconnect with the Christ figure.

It is impossible to convey in words what an encounter with the numinous might be like and on hearing about it the first reaction is usually one of disbelief and skepticism. There is, of course, no guarantee that one will have a numinous experience during Rebirthing, although it does happen more often than not.

Another woman, Elaine, I met at a past-life therapy training workshop where we were teamed up to give each other a session. When it was my turn to facilitate her process I asked her to very gently breathe the Rebirthing way. Towards the end of her session she encountered what she described as God, a being so brilliant, so kind and compassionate that it totally changed her image of God, which had been quite negative until then.

During Rebirthing sufficient pranic force and momentum will have been received by your body to enable it to flow through the whole of your being, cleansing and revitalizing it and releasing the slightest blockage in its path that has emerged during the session. That is when you can enter an 'altered' state of consciousness where a direct experience of the numinous becomes possible. Once you have been in the presence of this being of light or fire your consciousness can never return to its previous state of relative darkness.

We do not yet understand the forces involved. Alice Bailey speaks of 'that essential dynamic electric Fire which produces all there is, and is the sustaining, originating Cause and Source of all manifestation.' Whatever this energy is, it connects us to a spiritual force that is different from anything we have previously known. It is similar to but at the same time different from the state of bliss you might achieve in meditation or through yogic exercises. The only comparison anyone has ever made is with drug-induced altered states of consciousness.

I do not want to give the impression, however, that Rebirthing is an easy route to getting 'spaced out.' You may indeed get spaced out and will most likely experience altered states of consciousness, but first you need to do the breath-work. You will have to make the effort to breathe consciously, rhythmically and continuously for a period of time. You will have to learn a new skill and perhaps for the first time in your life make proper use of your lungs. You will also have to learn how to 'get out of your own way' and let a transpersonal process unfold. You will be encouraged to be curious about what the breath will do to you, what new experiences it may draw from the secret depths of your being. There is *never* any need to be afraid because what the breath cleanses out of your body-mind has already happened to you. Any disturbing scenarios, feelings or thoughts will simply disappear as you continue to breathe. The breath brings in a benevolent, loving, creative life force that is on your side – that is totally good and healing.

Many people, when they begin to feel the energy entering their bodies, compare it to electricity. Some people like the sensation and are profoundly moved by what seems to them to be a miracle. Others are frightened by the power, fearing that it will destroy something in them rather than heal. Such people like to be in total 'control' at all times, and the more powerful their position in the material world, the more difficult it seems to be for them to 'let go.' They will try to resist by thinking and worrying about all manner of things instead of relaxing and focusing on breathing.

As I am writing this (January 20, 1998), an article on Rebirthing has just appeared in Britain's *Daily Mail*. Dr Raj Persaud, a psychiatrist from a major London psychiatric hospital, who is also a journalist for the paper, went for a Rebirthing session in order to investigate the therapy. I was not surprised to read that he did not have a profound experience, as he was not able to relax. Whilst he was breathing he kept thinking about what the breath was doing, whether he was breathing too fast, whether it was dangerous and whether he would pass out. His bleeper went off twice during the session and he actually got up to answer it!

People who want to stay in control at all times, who start out with a skeptical attitude and are unable to allow themselves to open to new and unfamiliar experiences, need particularly firm but gentle guidance. The practitioner needs to bring them back repeatedly to the awareness of the breath and stop them from talking. Talking is a way of evading the issues that need to be raised to consciousness. When a thought comes in the client should be encouraged to just let it go, remind themselves that this is 'only thinking,' return to the breath and, above all, turn off the bleeper and the mobile! After a while their fear of loss of control will vanish, to be replaced by a trusting acceptance of the safety of the rhythm of the breathing.

FEAR OF CHANGE

The first thing that often emerges in a breathing session is resistance to change itself. You may say, 'But I want to change, I am yearning for change. I can't stand my life any longer. Anything must be better than this!' Well, yes and no. You may want your life to change, but in reality you only want it to be *better*. Change demands sacrifice, adaptation to new circumstances and a commitment to the unknown, for better *or* worse. If you can face the future despite your fears of what might be round the corner, you have already begun to shift away from the attitude of the dull masses who are always waiting for the better luck that might come tomorrow. A song from childhood comes to mind:

In the waiting room to the great fortune
there are a lot of people sitting around.
They have waited since yesterday for the fortune of tomorrow,
and live with wishes for the day after tomorrow,
But have forgotten that it is only today.
Oh, those poor, poor people.

It is not unusual for people to voice their or their partner's fears about the changes that might take place in their lives as a result of Rebirthing. Sometimes people have to come secretly without letting their partner know what they are doing. Sometimes a person is 'forbidden' by their partner to have sessions. Sometimes the very word 'Rebirthing' can stir up all manner of fears and issues, just as it did with me. These fears may be provoked by early memories of an event that changed life for ever and or of a defeat of some kind. There is nothing wrong with being afraid, as long as it does not become an obstacle to change. Fear can be a useful emotion, as when you are facing physical danger, for example. It is only when it paralyses you into dull passivity or makes you over-aggressive that it will work against your own good.

Fear in Rebirthing sessions might manifest as a sudden desire to go to sleep, as a feeling of dizziness or faintness, or as a reluctance to breathe. Some people suddenly feel that breathing in this way is silly, that they look ridiculous lying there with their mouths half open, and they start to laugh. But with encouragement from the therapist they will continue to breathe until the scene changes, the dizziness goes and the head clears, and the laughter perhaps turns into tears.

Another typical symptom of resistance to the incoming energy is tightness in various parts of the body, frequently accompanied by a cold sensation, either in those parts or in the whole body. Anger is another way resistance to change can show itself. This may be experienced as lack of trust in, and irritation with, the therapist, or as a feeling of insecurity about the breathing itself.

. A frequent situation that arises early on during Rebirthing therapy is the physical reliving of one's birth. The enormous change involved in emerging from nine months or so inside a watery, warm, dark and relatively safe womb into a bright and noisy environment that hurts the lungs is a trauma for any baby. So, when the breathing starts to stimulate this early pre-verbal experience, you at first have no idea what it is all about and may fear that you will be crushed to death, so you will try to resist with all your might. There is no way that you would want to go through that again. Some people actually cry out: 'Oh no, I couldn't survive it again!' When I ask what they mean, they don't know. If you have been breathing correctly, though, and you have got this far in the session, you will be on your way. From now on there is no turning back. Your Rebirth has begun.

As you continue to breathe, the power that enters on the incoming breath will gradually increase and move you forward, through the experience that you have been resisting, either mentally or physically, until you finally reach a stage of at-one-ment within yourself and with the world. This final stage of a total merging with all there is can only come about after you have worked through your initial resistance, after you have made the effort to complete the full Rebirthing cycle.

This is not to say that it cannot be easy. In fact, whether or not a breathing session goes smoothly depends a great deal on one's capacity to hold a *dual consciousness* whilst undergoing the various experiences. By 'dual consciousness' I mean the ability to fully enter into the experience while also knowing that you are releasing blocking and harmful memories. If you can achieve this, you are more likely to be able to keep the breathing cycle going smoothly until the experience has been 'breathed out.' It is like *watching* yourself having the experience. This will in no way detract from the intensity of the situation, but you will not add to the struggle by resisting its release. Remember that what is happening in the sessions has already happened to you in the past and you are now letting go of it. By being afraid of what you need to let go of you are only adding new fear to what is already there. A skilful Rebirther will lead you confidently through this part, supporting you and helping you confront that fear.

An important point to bear in mind is that whatever you are able to do in a session you will also be able to do in life. If you can make an almost superhuman effort to keep breathing when what you really feel compelled to do is drop off to sleep (which so often happens), you will find that obstacles in your everyday life will also be dealt with with much greater ease in the future. It just 'sort of happens' that way.

Sometimes I ask people after a few sessions how they are coping now with problems and frequently the answer will be that they do not know because no actual problems have arisen of late. Kirsty, for example, came to see me because she felt unhappy and unloved and because of a variety of physical symptoms, including chronic migraines and blockages in her abdomen, which had been operated on several times, as well as extreme pains in her neck. She was in a near-permanent state of anger and frustration and unhappiness. After her third session I happened to ask her how she was getting on with her husband. Her response, which did not surprise me but nevertheless made me smile, was: 'Oh, I don't know. There hasn't really been any conflict between us lately, so I haven't had a chance to find out.'

THE MISSING LINK

It is important to remember that the breath only ever brings to the surface, and therefore into consciousness, something that you do not already know. Even if you have had years of other types of therapy, as I had, Rebirthing will seek out those memories that have remained unreachable by any other approach. These memories lie deeply embedded in your cellular structure, where they live an autonomous life, affecting you mostly negatively, and because they are unconscious they cannot be transformed. The following example will illustrate this.

Irma is in her late twenties. She has three young children, two of whom have not yet started school. On rainy days she used to find herself stuck at home with them, which she very much resented. She would get depressed the moment she opened her eyes in the morning and could hear the rain beating against the window. She would then be unable to play with her children or give them any attention, feeling too depressed to even want to get out of bed. She put this down to the fact that they were all stuck indoors, that she was bored because there was nothing to do and that she was literally 'under the weather.' As soon as the skies cleared, her moods lifted.

In her very first breathing session, which was on a bright and sunny day, she went back to a time when she could hear rain lashing against a window. I encouraged her to explore this further and asked her where she was. An early childhood memory came flooding back into her consciousness with such realism and force that she started to actually relive it. She began to shiver and her legs shook. 'I am about two years old. It's cold and it's raining hard outside,' she said in a small voice, 'and I am all alone! I am sitting on a chair underneath a window which is too high for me to see out of. My sisters are at school and my mother has gone out to the shops without me because of the weather. She told me to just sit very still and that she will be back soon. And that is what I am doing now, sitting very still. I am very frightened and I daren't move but I am shaking like a leaf. Then my mother comes back, says, "Hello," and carries on as before. She has noticed nothing and I am unable to tell her.' She wept quietly for a while and then the memory was gone. From that day Irma never again suffered from depression when it rained.

This is a very clear example of how when a 'sick memory' is removed from the cellular structure by the cleansing breath it ceases to cause problems and can do us no more harm. Irma had been too young to remember the event consciously, but her body remembered each time she was trapped inside when it was raining.

The following example also deals with the removal of sick memory, but in this case there was no specific event in early childhood that had given rise to it. Emma had suffered from depression for many years. An attractive, intelligent mother of two, she had been in therapy for twelve years. Each morning she awoke with a feeling of inner doom, finding it hard to face yet another day. Had it not been for the fact that she needed to get her children ready for school she would have spent most of the day in bed. Her five-year-old son had not yet learned to talk and no one knew why. The general medical opinion was that he had a neurological disorder but no evidence for this could be produced. Emma sounded as though she had given up hope of him ever making progress. Her whole being had a feeling of deadness about it. She would often simply say 'Yes' or 'No' or shrug when asked a question. She was full of self-doubt and felt all her troubles, including her depression, were her own fault. When I asked her what her most negative feelings were about herself, she said without hesitation, 'I am ugly. Nobody wants me.'

It turned out that after a fairly amicable divorce she had become involved with a man with whom she did not feel secure, as he would not commit himself to her, only saw her when it suited him and disappeared for weeks at a time. When he reappeared he expected to pick up the relationship where he had left it. She was supporting him financially from time to time and he had a key to her house. 'If I didn't have such low self-esteem I wouldn't see this man again,' she told me at our first meeting. But at the same time she could not imagine life without him.

It was apparent from the background details Emma gave me that she had suffered a great deal as a child, which might have been the cause of her depression. Overall, though, she did not tell me anything during our initial session that she had not already discussed with her previous therapists. As she had come specifically for Rebirthing I wrote down her details but did not try to do any process work (i.e. look for ways of healing) by talking about her problems. Instead we went straight into a breathing session.

What transpired in the very first session was as much of a surprise to me as it was to her. I would have expected early childhood traumas to emerge but instead Emma experienced in minute detail giving birth to a very primitive baby while she herself was a 'cave-human.' She could feel the odd bone structure of her skull and the strange shapes of her nose and her mouth, which felt too big for her face. She could see in clearest detail the interior of the cave with its red wall paintings. *And she knew what to do!* She knew without assistance how to give birth.

Whether this was a past-life experience or whether Emma was symbolically giving birth to herself is not important. An experience has value in itself and does not need to be interpreted; its healing power will do its work just the same. As it was, Emma went through all the physical sensations of giving birth inside the cave. She was acutely aware of the 'baby' pressing down on her lower back, causing a great deal of pain. Then the breath moved her swiftly through into the final stage when she, by now in ecstasy, gave birth to a new being. This birth, with its intensity, an experience that is difficult to express in words, had a most profoundly emotional and meaningful effect on her.

I have encountered this again and again. When women give birth in a Rebirthing session they are overcome by the most powerful feelings of love and reverence for the miracle of the new human soul. (It is not uncommon for men also to experience themselves as women giving birth. Their sensations and emotions seem identical to those of women. Men can be just as overwhelmed and touched and transformed by the act of birth-giving.) If a woman has children, she may not have been able to experience their birth in this way at the time, but the body remembers every time, even when the mother's trauma was severe or when the birth took place in another life. There is a part in each and every one of us that is untouched by outer circumstances, that is inscrutable and inviolable. To reach this part usually means years of study and meditation, perhaps combined with special diets. And even then there is no guarantee that we 'get there.' Life is very complex and the obstacles that lie in the path to Self-realization are numerous indeed. A Buddhist would say that it is our karma, the effects of past actions, that prevents us from seeing and living life as it is in essence.

When Emma experienced that birth in an altered state of consciousness and at this higher, purer and essential level, she also became aware of the presence of her grandmother, who had been dead for some years and who seemed to be acting as a midwife. She had been very important to Emma during childhood, providing the only stability and security she had ever known. After giving birth, Emma the cave-woman walked out onto the African veldt, carrying her baby as if it weighed almost nothing, and felt a strength inside herself that was supernatural.

Emma understood this experience to be a spontaneous glimpse of a past life and found great strength in what had transpired. She felt that this would now help her to bear the burden of her own children. Afterwards she could barely talk about what she had just been through. Words just do not suffice when describing experiences of this nature. But she did say, 'It was incredibly beautiful and helped me to link to a more primitive and wholesome side of my nature which had been blocked.' She also noticed that the chronic lower back pain she had suffered from for years had disappeared. Three months earlier she had had an operation on her back and only three weeks before on her right knee, leaving her in considerable discomfort. Now, all pain had gone. Indeed, throughout the session she had been aware of a deep healing process taking place. I am now convinced that there is a deeper level within the body-memory that must be reached in order to bring about complete healing. Rebirthing provides this link between the known and the unknown dimensions of human nature.

When I saw Emma for her second session she felt physically much better in terms of energy and alertness, but it was not until after her ninth session that she woke up one morning and realized that she was no longer depressed. The clouds had lifted; a new life-affirming attitude was born. Her son had started talking at last and she had separated from her boyfriend. She is now training to become a counselor and is already doing valuable work.

Whilst Emma removed 'sick memory' from her body-mind she sometimes experienced it physically through bodily sensations such as tightness and pain in various parts. Memory is stored in our bodies somewhere, somehow; one theory is that it becomes embedded in our cellular structure in the form of chemicals. As the Rebirthing breath works deeply into our cells, cleansing, vitalizing and regenerating, these chemicals are released and with them the memories. As we continue with the breathing cycle, at first reliving these memories and then releasing them, they go for good and can no longer have power over us and do us harm.

As you become more and more the person you are meant to be, without all that clutter from the past, you start to take better care of yourself. This will be reflected in the food you eat and the exercise you take. You develop new relationships and interests and a greater sense of life-purpose. You begin to want to give something back to the world. You may start training for a new profession, take up painting or emigrate. Sooner or later your life's work will start, when you are ready, in however small a way. Your life will start to change as if of its own accord. You will meet the right person; get the right job offer; your partner, for no apparent reason, will become more considerate towards you; people will enjoy your company more. You will become aware that you are not only a body with a mind and feelings, but also a living soul, and that life can be lived more joyfully and abundantly.

 CHANGE YOUR LIFE IN
TWENTY HOURS

*The most splendid products of the mind will also vanish if the
smallest obstacle obstructs the unconscious activity of the soul
governing the blood flow to the heart or regulating the phases
of breathing.*
C. G. Carus (1789–1869)

I have trained in and have received various forms of therapy over
the past twenty-five years, but none of them achieve anything like
the results encountered in Rebirthing – and none of them work so
fast. Yet this therapy has been criticized perhaps more than any
other and always by people who have never had an experience of
it, or at least not a proper one, with a well-trained practitioner who
is also a psychotherapist.

Some of the greatest critics are actually therapists from other
disciplines. When I mention that I am a Rebirther eyes glaze over and
grow cold, and bodies stiffen. When I talk about what Rebirthing can
actually do for a person, I get the impression I am committing a sin.
Mention of contact with the numinous is considered nothing less

than blasphemous. One senior therapist, during a recent discussion, thought that if people really did get something out of Rebirthing it was because they had already prepared for it by doing a great deal of work on themselves. Another, equally senior, asserted that any break-through, any mystical experience encountered during breathing work could be nothing more than a temporary phenomenon, leaving the person untouched by it. Yet another found it totally unbelievable that work on oneself could proceed with any speed at all.

At this discussion there were five Rebirthers present and one therapist from another discipline who had never had a Rebirthing session. To my dismay no one seemed to have the slightest idea what I was talking about and, therefore, either remained silent or dismissed my descriptions of what I had encountered through the breath as totally improbable.

One person compared what I was describing to meditation and although I knew what she meant, the results of Rebirthing are not at all the same as those of meditation. However, she was interested enough to ask a few questions, one being whether Rebirthing could become addictive. Could one perhaps become dependent on it? I can assure any reader who has the same question in mind that it is no more addictive than meditation or regular exercise, or reading for that matter. I have never come across anyone who is actually addicted to it.

It appears, though, that the idea of Rebirthing makes people feel queasy, as it did me at first. People have said to me that they would not trust anyone enough to totally lose control in their presence. When I tell them that they can get up and walk out any time during a session, they are surprised. They might be a bit giddy, mind you, if they were to walk out in the middle of a breathing cycle. Only one of my clients has ever done that. This was a middle-aged woman who arrived for her session at six o'clock in the evening, all dressed up to go out to dinner. About halfway through the breathing cycle she looked at her watch, gave a yelp and rushed out of the door, explaining to me, as she ran, that she was due to meet someone half an hour ago. Needless to say her first experience was not a good one.

In a world where people are too busy to give much attention to their inner lives, where everyone wants a quick fix and where the demand is for instant gratification, entering into long-term therapy does not appeal. There is an urgency today for the human race to hurry and grow psycho-spiritually, as if we were running out of time. Spiritual growth has become a growth industry. The enormous expansion of schools and colleges that now offer courses in alternative therapies could not have come about had there not first been a demand for it. Everyone wants to *get there* more quickly and, hopefully, without too much effort and expense. The choices now on offer are wide and varied and can be confusing, but the common purpose is to help you along your path more quickly, to provide relief from pain without having to endure more pain, and to balance mind and body. It is the urgency and readiness of the human soul (for the soul is the force of evolution itself) to advance along the path of individuation – the path of return to the source – more rapidly that has attracted this wave of short-cut therapy.

As a brief therapy, which may only last a few weeks, Rebirthing has no equal. Other forms of brief therapy are usually designed to get people back to living a 'normal' life in society as quickly as possible and to help them cope with everyday difficulties. Rebirthing goes much further. Its aim is not to help you deal better with the demands of the world you live in or to calm you or make you a nicer person. *The aim of Rebirthing therapy is first and foremost to help you become more of the person that you are in your true essence.*

Rebirthing offers a short-cut that bypasses your ordinary thinking function. Instead, the Rebirthing breath, as it courses through your body, offers you the direct experience of a spiritual force. During Rebirthing you are breathing in spirit, enabling your body to receive an extraordinarily vast amount of spiritual energy. Each time you breathe the full cycle your soul is nourished by the stuff that life is made of, or, as Alice Bailey put it in *Treatise on the Seven Rays*, Vol. I., 'The spirit in man is producing an evolutionary development of the soul, through the use of matter.'

Every time you go through a Rebirthing experience you witness the interplay of spirit and matter. As the incoming energy interacts with your body a drama unfolds. The body resists at first with all its might. The energy blockages thus manifested have often been lying dormant within our being for many lifetimes. The physical struggle to let go of these can be tremendous and very painful, but the relief and joy when finally the body gives way to the flow of new life-energy are worth all the struggle.

We do not yet fully understand what actually happens inside our bodies during this process. In *The Doors of Perception* Aldous Huxley suggests that 'each one of us may be capable of manufacturing a chemical, minute doses of which are known to cause profound changes in consciousness.' Half an hour after Huxley took the drug mescaline he became aware of 'a slow dance of golden lights.' Although in Rebirthing time factors can vary enormously according to the individual, it also takes approximately half an hour for visionary experiences to begin. In the past these experiences have been dismissed as hallucinatory and, therefore, of no importance. Today they are more often regarded as also real, but belonging to another dimension of human existence.

Breathing oneself into this Otherworld has, of course, tremendous advantages. Besides the brilliant visions and the beings of light and love that are frequently encountered, there is the additional benefit of cellular cleansing and cellular regeneration without any stress on the liver from the use of drugs or strain on the heart (the breathing can be practiced as gently or as powerfully as one chooses) and nervous system. What one does not encounter, however, in a Rebirthing session, during which the eyes usually remain shut, is the supernatural luminosity of the surrounding *physical* world, where, as D. Bradshaw in the Introduction to Huxley's *Doors of Perception* described it, 'the "divine source of all existence" is evident in a vase of flowers.'

What does happen, though, is the release of energy blockages in the body-mind. After each session you feel that something has gone, as if it had just sort of slipped out of your body with great ease. You may feel relaxed, but it is a special kind of relaxation, a relaxation that makes your body feel totally at one and in tune with your mind. You feel no separation either within yourself or from the world around you.

Once something has been breathed out of your body, it will undergo a purification by fire and, thus transformed, will enter the common atmosphere. By expiring (and we must remember that there is not only inspiration but also expiration), we offer our suffering up to a higher power. As we surrender ourselves with each exhale, blocked energy is surrendered too, leaving us free to form new energy patterns, changing our inner world, which in turn influences our outer world.

You can change your life in twenty hours, that is, ten two-hour sessions. It may of course take less time than that. My own life changed completely within a relatively short period after only one session and the majority of people also see an improvement in their lives from the start. But ten sessions usually suffice to clear the energy channels of the body of unwanted matter from the past, creating an environment in which your soul can prosper. Rebirthing acts so quickly because it goes straight to where a problematical event has become an unconscious memory, a complex or a disease, and effectively releases it.

The case of Georgia will serve as a simple illustration. She had been suffering from an ulcer for many years. During her first session she relived a frightening scenario when she was about four years old and was sitting on her mother's lap. Her mother had just finished breastfeeding her younger sister.

'Now you,' she said, 'you have some of this, too,' and offered the little girl her breast.

Georgia was absolutely horrified and screamed, 'I am a big girl now, please don't make me.' She had a struggle with her mother and escaped the humiliation.

During Rebirthing she vividly relived the horror of this experience, her disgust of the breast and the repulsive thought of her mother's warm milk. As she did so she could feel her stomach contract and the pain increasing. I encouraged her to stay with the discomfort until the breath, of its own accord, passed through the area, penetrating the old pain and all the sensations and negative emotions that she had felt up to that point in connection with the incident. She completed the cycle calm and quiet and aware that the memory had left her, and very shortly after this session her ulcer disappeared. This is a good example of what can happen when spiritual energy flows without hindrance to the part of the body that needs healing. That part responds by releasing the block and the illness disappears.

Some people, of course, are very skeptical and will try to sabotage any changes that want to take place. Either they stop coming for further sessions or excuse away any changes that *have* taken place by saying that they would have happened anyway. One of my clients, in the middle of her third session, said: 'Is it good to remember all these things from childhood?' She had been listening to a radio program that morning warning people about false memory syndrome and now felt she couldn't trust her own process any more. Another woman, also whilst in the middle of her breathing cycle, wondered whether she was 'betraying Jesus.' When I asked her what she meant she said that her Church was against anything that the Bible does not teach. But luckily she soon burst out laughing.

This is not to say that Rebirthing does not work for skeptics. A respected psychiatrist from a teaching hospital in London, for example, who had only come out of curiosity, was so intrigued when the breathing took him into a blissful, ecstatic, altered state of consciousness that he booked in for the whole course, even though it meant rearranging his work schedule. But he avoided mentioning our work to his colleagues for fear of being ridiculed.

This doctor showed a healthy skepticism but remained open to change. Skepticism that does not allow for experimentation and the inclusion of new experiences and attitudes, on the other hand, is simply short-sighted sabotage and psychic bullying. Such skeptics have big 'no-sayers' inside them that destroy anything that might lead to the unhinging of the status quo. They should perhaps start off with some straightforward talking therapy in order to get to know this no-sayer better. A no-sayer is a distortion of wisdom who appears to know what is best for us, but in reality is afraid of possible changes and losing power. If one could put one's inner no-sayer on ice, so to speak, for the duration of each session, the inherent wisdom that resides within each person's Self would be given a chance to emerge.

Our psyches are naturally conservative, of course. Every change means that some parts of our nature need to be transformed or sacrificed. Nothing wants to die, yet every change demands a death.

If you are strong enough to breathe the consciously connected Rebirthing way your life *will* change, and in a relatively short time. But change can be positive. Christopher, for example, aged forty, left his job as a personnel officer of a large company after only one Rebirthing session and enrolled in a university degree course in media studies. His secret ambition had always been to be involved in show business in some way but he had never felt that he had the confidence or the right to do something about it. He recently wrote to me after his graduation ball, at which he had to give the after-dinner speech, which, he said, went very well. Now he is hoping to find work, which I have no doubt he will be offered in next to no time.

If you have a secret ambition, you too may find that Rebirthing will help you achieve it. You will certainly find yourself becoming healthier, more energetic, relaxed, open to transformation and, most importantly, aware that you are a living soul that has a consciousness, power, purpose and will of its own. Each Rebirthing session will bring you closer to this source of your being until you will be able to fully co-operate with the way of the soul, whatever this may mean for you. It may express itself in the work you are doing, in the way you relate to others, in your dreams or in any changes you may want to make in your life. You may develop an irresistible urge to alter your professional life, leave a relationship that serves no further purpose or meet your soul-mate and start the work that awaits you both. You will still encounter difficulties, but they can become stepping-stones instead of hindrances.

As with any journey, if you want to go somewhere you need to know where to start from. You need to know where you are right here and now. Then you can map out your route. Once a conscious connection has been made, the steps you need to take in order to co-operate with your soul are unavoidable. But you will take these steps gladly and without hesitation when the time is right, and ripe, and you will trust that all will be well.

# 4 EACH SESSION IS UNIQUE

When the mirror of your heart becomes clear and pure,
you'll behold images which are outside this world.
You will see the image and the image-Maker,
both the carpet of the spiritual expanse
and the One who spreads it.
Rumi

What actually happens during a session? In my years of experience as a Rebirther no two sessions have ever been identical. What happens depends entirely on the individual and my interaction with them. Whilst I can make general statements about the length of the average session and how one should breathe, it is impossible to say in advance what might occur. I never fail to be surprised by the interesting material people have buried in their unconscious minds, and by the extraordinarily detailed memories that reach back to intra-uterine existence and beyond. On many occasions I have been blissfully entertained; on others I have felt sad, angry or wept with the client. Most of all I have developed a deep respect for the profound and enormous power of the Rebirthing breath. This simple breath has the power to bring about life-changing transformations that affect people positively for the rest of their lives.

We tend to forget that if we stop breathing we shall die within a very few minutes. The breath is the essential carrier of life, as Jung tells us in his commentary to *The Secret of the Golden Flower*. Life in this sense, though, does not only mean being alive, but also living a life that is *inspired* with purpose and direction. This spiritual purpose and direction is the most important gift that Rebirthing can give us. Without it we flounder and come under what Gurdjieff calls the 'law of accident,' when just about anything can happen to us, not necessarily what is the choosing of our soul.

The idea that spiritual energy is always available, that we can breathe it in and that it can free us to live the life that is meant for us is an exciting one. It brings hope to many people who have already tried to break through to what they sense is their *real* Self by practicing yoga or meditation or through the use of drugs. Graham, a client who had tried various drugs throughout the sixties and seventies, exclaimed, on reaching the visionary part of his session, 'My God, this is like LSD, only better!' The final words of an enthusiastic article by Brendan O'Connor, a journalist from the Irish *Sunday Independent*, who came to me 'to bury Rebirthing rather than to praise it,' read: 'All I can say is that Rebirthing is better than any drug I've ever heard of.' He now appears regularly in a weekly satirical news comedy show on television.

Each Rebirth is a unique experience every single time for each individual. No two people have exactly the same problems or the same past, and no two people have the same needs. During the session it is not the therapist who decides what an individual needs but their own psyche, their true Self. So, what transpires during a session is exactly what is required for that particular person at that particular time.

THE INITIAL INTERVIEW

Whilst there is no such thing as a typical session, with a few exceptions most Rebirthing therapy will follow a certain pattern. At the first meeting a thorough case-history is taken, with an emphasis on past traumatic events, accidents, illnesses and major turning-points. It is not uncommon during the initial interview for someone to talk about a major trauma that they have never discussed with anyone else before. The relief can be instant. For most people the most traumatic incident in their lives will have been their birth, so particular attention is paid to this. The release of the birth trauma from the body-mind memory is always a breakthrough.

Next we examine the present life situation: what makes life a problem right now? I call this 'tilling the soil' – letting a little light and space into the density and darkness of the inner world. Quite often just by discussing their current difficulties, people experience a change in attitude and are ready for further exploration. But the 'presenting issue' – the life situation that brings a person into therapy in the first place – whilst being the motivating force, is very rarely the real cause of the difficulties in their life.

MOTIVATION

Each person who undertakes Rebirthing will be motivated, of course. Motivation is what gets you *moving*. Without it nothing happens. Any kind of crisis, any kind of rational or irrational reason, can be the motivation for starting Rebirthing sessions, but the greatest motivator of all, perhaps the only one, is pain. Whatever it is that makes you feel frustrated, hopeless, despairing or stuck, it is pain that motivates you to make it stop. I am talking here about the kind of pain that you experience when life is not fulfilling, when you feel that something has gone fundamentally wrong. 'Life is not supposed to be like this,' you may say, as I did. 'There must be more to it than this.' This is *divine discontent*, the discontent you feel because you are not connected to your soul or to some other essential part of yourself.

There is built into the human psyche a deep vision of moving forward and upward – an archetypal sense of somewhere to get to. Most people do not know what or where this somewhere is, and doubt whether it even exists, but they strive towards it just the same, their spiritual longing disguised as desire for material possessions or status or relationship. Our pain is our reminder, our conscience, the Jiminy Cricket of our souls. It reminds us that all is not as it should be and that things must change in order for us to find our path, our vocation and the life that *is* meant for us.

Some people, feeling this pain, have already been in more conventional therapy for a while but come to Rebirthing because they want something more, something to put them in touch with parts of themselves that they didn't already know, parts that a typical talking therapy could not reach.

The analysis of childhood, for example, is very useful and often necessary, but it would be wrong to assume that all our problems stem from childhood. Some people have had quite a happy childhood yet are anxious, agitated or angry. Others have had to endure the most awful abuse and suffering, either through circumstance – as in war – or through illness, the loss of a loved one or the cruelty of a parent, yet develop into wise, strong and philosophical adults. It would be a great mistake therefore to look for all life's problems in one's relationship to one's parents, siblings and other members of the family. What can emerge, though, through psychotherapy, is a certain *pattern tendency*, that is, an inclination to act in certain ways, to attract certain situations or to be introverted or extroverted. The exploration of these patterns, making them conscious, understanding them and taking responsibility for them, can contribute much to a person's recovery from childhood experiences.

But this is by no means the whole story. In many cases the core problem remains untouched. A deep inner pain, a discontent, remains. Rebirthing is able to uncover the 'story behind the story' and frequently provides a 'cure,' in the form of a change in attitude, in just one session.

Angela, for example, who lives in South Africa, had only one session with me, but it totally changed her life. She was motivated by the fact that she was working so hard expanding her design company that she was not having any fun. She would find herself sitting alone in her beautiful garden at weekends, unable to enjoy her hard-earned riches. After her Rebirth she set about changing her life radically to have more time for the things she really enjoyed. She now spends a fraction of her time in the office and instead travels the world looking for artifacts and attending courses on various subjects, including ethnic art and spiritual topics.

THE TECHNIQUE

At the start of the first Rebirthing session I briefly check on the most recent events in the client's life to see whether anything has changed since the initial interview, for it often happens that there is an energy shift between that and the first Rebirthing session. Frequently important occurrences are precipitated, as if the psyche were preparing for the next step forward. Then the client lies down on a mattress under a blanket or duvet. We are now ready to commence the breathing.

The Rebirthing breath is simple and safe to practice. It is so simple, in fact, that you need to try it out for yourself in order to believe the claims made about it, and it is so powerful that it is able to change lives quickly and with apparent ease.

The breath is drawn up through your feet, which should not be crossed over, into the top of your chest. You aim for maximum inhale, filling your lungs to capacity. You do *not* push the exhale but rather relax it, allowing the rib-cage and diaphragm to collapse. This pushes the air out without effort. This is in theory not difficult, but it is surprising how many people find it almost impossible at first and need a lot of assistance and practice. Here is an exercise so you can try it out for yourself.

Exercise

Note: If you are suffering from a particular illness or health condition consult your health practitioner before embarking on any specific breathing practice.

Try twenty breaths now as an initial exercise. *Unless you have done this type of breathing before, go no further than twenty breaths until you are able to go a full cycle with a trained practitioner.* You may practice these twenty breaths a few times a day to get the hang of it.

Lie or sit comfortably, shut your eyes and breathe in through your mouth, imagining that you are drawing the breath up from your feet into your upper chest, as if you were trying to touch the insides of the top of your shoulders with the breath. Then, without a pause, relax your exhale. Don't control it, hold it or push it, but simply let it go as if it were falling away of its own accord. Imagine that you are dissolving with it as it leaves you. Mentally, but without any physical effort, direct the exhale back to your feet along the outside of your body, allowing your diaphragm to collapse. Then, without pause, pull the breath up again through your feet into the top of your chest and, again without a pause, relax the exhale back to your feet and so on. Do *not* extend your abdomen.

The three most important points to remember are:

- With eyes shut, breathe in and out through your mouth with the emphasis on the inhale. Do not alternate mouth and nose breathing. Imagine that you are drawing the breath up through your feet into the top of your chest. Draw in a little more breath than during normal breathing. Let your lungs stretch a bit.
- Relax the exhale. Do not push it, force it or form it. Imagine that your throat is wide and open like a tunnel.
- Keep the breath connected without pauses between inhale and exhale. As soon as you have exhaled, pull the breath up again

from your feet. You do not need to exhale all the way if it seems to you that your exhale is rather long.

I repeat: the emphasis needs to be on the inhale. The exhale falls away naturally and the breath needs to assume a natural rhythm and continuous circuit.

You can adjust the speed at which you breathe to suit your own comfort. As long as you breathe in with extra effort with an open throat and a sense that your lungs are filling to capacity, the speed is immaterial. Some people I have Rebirthed have been so frail and exhausted that they could only breathe very shallowly. Even so, because the breath was connected and continuous, they could accumulate enough *prana* or life force to achieve a Rebirth, and felt revitalized and strengthened afterwards.

This form of breathing will not only establish a connection to your spiritual Self, nourish your soul and free your creativity, but it is also a useful technique in all kinds of different situations to effect relaxation, reflection and inspiration and to enhance the imagination.

As a session progresses the rhythm will become more natural and smooth until it will seem that the breath is breathing you. When this stage has been reached your subtle bodies will have been reorganized and brought into full alignment with your body's vital energy centers (the chakras). You will know that this is happening because you can actually feel it. If you have been breathing correctly and for long enough your body will feel completely integrated and at peace.

During breathing you may experience a tight jaw if you do not relax your exhale but push or blow it. This can also happen, although much more rarely, even if your exhale is relaxed. As children, our natural expression, especially that of anger and frustration, is often suppressed because we are told to keep quiet and not to speak until we are spoken to or, perhaps worse still, we are ridiculed for what we do say if we dare to speak. In other words, children are often told to keep their mouths shut. This can easily lead to gritted teeth and clenched jaws. Every dentist has many stories to tell. When I first started working as a Rebirther I was amazed at how many people have these tight jaws. If you hold on to tension in your jaws your whole body will be tense. Just try it, now, and you will feel that the tightness produces a reflex right down to your feet. Therefore, much of my attention in the first session is given to gently loosening this area.

But paying attention to a particular area does not mean controlling the session. The material, the stories, the pains and sorrows that emerge must be allowed to be released. This process can be facilitated tremendously by encouraging relaxation in various parts of the body. At the end of the session there will be much more flexibility in those parts and a feeling that they have been gently bathed or 'lubricated.'

A few minutes after starting the breathing the incoming energy will begin to affect the body and produce subtle changes. There may be a fine tingling sensation throughout the body, or dizziness, or tightness in the head or chest. The feelings vary from person to person and there is absolutely no guideline as to what might happen. The best policy is to accept anything and everything from now on. You might suddenly become freezing cold and need extra covers or very hot and throw off the blanket. You might want to burst out laughing without knowing why. The important thing is to keep the breath going. The sensations and emotions will change of their own accord and in time disappear altogether.

As a therapist, my most important contribution at this stage is to ensure that you keep on breathing in the right manner until you assume a natural rhythm and the breath comes automatically and easily. Your task is to use all your available will-power and keep making the effort until you break through your body's resistance.

The first thing the breath brings up in most people is the inertia typically associated with blockages in the body's energy field.

The effect of this is that one wants to go to sleep, that one cannot go on, feels it is all too hard, etc. These are the same kind of feelings that we experience when confronted with tasks or challenges that we have no enthusiasm for or interest in or that we lack the confidence or ability to tackle.

At this point my encouragement and support are vital. I will make little suggestions throughout the session regarding the pace or length of the breath. I may also give instructions about exhaling in different ways in order to facilitate the release of energy blockages.

But essentially it is your story that is beginning to unfold. Those bodily sensations hold memories and as you tune into what they are trying to say, whole scenarios from the past can suddenly erupt and early traumas such as birth, accidents, illnesses and emotional pain can be released. By now you are in an altered state of consciousness, induced by the breath, and although you may be reliving painful memories, you are at the same time also observing yourself doing so. The experience will be deep and profound, but you will always be aware of what is happening to you.

This process of bringing to the surface past memories from body and mind and releasing them with the exhale will continue for as long as it needs to. Gradually the breathing will become deeper and easier, the lungs will open wider and you will begin to feel warm and comfortable. At this stage I might suggest that you breathe normally, relax, sink into the mattress and allow yourself to drop off to sleep. This is what I call a 'yoga sleep.' Your breathing becomes very shallow, almost stopping altogether, and you lose awareness of your surroundings for a few minutes. You have entered the 'void,' that state of 'no-thingness,' no sensation and no consciousness in the normal sense of the word. You will return to everyday awareness of your own accord, usually with a feeling of lightness and floating.

It is at this stage that you may become aware of patterns of intense colour, of bright lights, of numinous beings or of persons long dead with whom you had a close relationship. The experiences at this stage are very similar in content, intensity and spiritual power to near-death experiences – an encounter with a sacred or spiritual dimension. A frequent occurrence is the appearance of a very bright light that does not hurt the eyes.

People often start breathing deeply again at this point, as if they know that the breath can help them to get closer to the light, and frequently they will 'enter' the light or merge with it. This is one of the most profound and powerful things that can happen. To bring the session to a close, I play soft evocative music.

Inspiration

When you are breathing it is also immensely helpful to be aware that you are connecting to a life force far greater than yourself. Breathing is *inspiration* and as we are being inspired creative ideas come to us out of the blue. We have not thought them up or worked them out. They just present themselves of their own accord.

During one of my earliest sessions, when I was still a trainee, I had a powerful vision of the sun, moon and all the nine planets from outside the solar system, beyond the farthest planet, Pluto. I could see the shape and details of Saturn's rings, mighty Jupiter and brilliant Venus with the most amazing clarity and in most vivid colors. The whole spectacle of the drama of the rotating universe was taking place right there in front of me within the limitless dimensions of my inner space.

'I can write my book now!' I exclaimed. There seemed to be no reason why I should connect this inner vision with writing a book. But there it was, the thought that came out of nowhere.

I could have explored this further, but unfortunately the man who was assisting me at the time was not into exploring the meaning of thoughts, ideas or visions. 'Just let go, Deike,' he said a little impatiently. 'Surrender!' I was disappointed that he did not honor what was happening to me, but much of Rebirthing is only about 'breathing and letting go' (though this is not the way I work). Many practitioners have no training in psychotherapy and do not know what to do with the emerging material. Nevertheless, the image has stayed with me, like many others similar in power and impact. These are among the great gifts you receive during Rebirthing and they always have a transforming quality about them and are of great significance.

Breathing the Rebirthing way is never boring. Each session is different. Internal seeing is brilliantly enhanced. Colored patterns, lights and strange beings all join in the unfolding drama and long-forgotten memories from this and other dimensions flood back into consciousness. Each Rebirth is an initiation in the sense that each leads to an expansion of consciousness. It needs spirit to ignite the spirit within you – only fire can ignite fire – and breathing in this way is the easiest, most powerful and soul-infusing way to do this.

To illustrate the vast variety of what can happen in a Rebirthing session, here are four examples.

Fear of Public Places

Marcia was the first person I ever Rebirthed outside my training program. I had hesitated at first over using this method with my regular therapy clients, but I had just finished my training and had not yet begun to seek out a special clientele for Rebirthing. Marcia had been coming to see me for hourly sessions on a weekly basis for a couple of years, mainly for talking and dream therapy, but occasionally we also included guided imagery. One morning she was late, which was unusual for her. When she finally arrived she seemed agitated and upset. 'I nearly didn't come,' she said with a haunted look on her face. 'I have been having these strange feelings lately and am afraid of leaving the house in case I fall or something. I cannot explain it, it's totally irrational, but I feel dizzy all the time, as if I were floating. It took all my will-power not to tele-phone you and cancel.'

'I am glad you came,' I said encouragingly. 'Just sit down and take a deep breath.'

She proceeded to tell me about the difficulty she had been having of late in stepping beyond her front door. There was nothing in Marcia's history that could be regarded as a trigger for this fear. My guess was that a pre-verbal or past-life memory was emerging. As we sat and talked I was wondering whether this might perhaps be an opportunity to work with the breath. I asked Marcia if she would like to try a gentle breathing exercise for relaxation. She agreed without hesitation.

I invited her to lie down on the floor and, sitting beside her, placed a hand lightly on her upper chest and instructed her to breathe in a connected circular direction. It was not long before her body started to go numb. Understandably, she was frightened, but I remembered from my training that numbness means that there is an energy blockage in the body and that one needs to keep on breathing until it is dissolved. So all I did at this stage was to encourage her to keep breathing. Within minutes she had become rigid and freezing cold and could no longer talk as her mouth, too, had become paralyzed. Her breathing became labored and she had to make a tremendous effort to keep up the rhythm.

Then she became aware of something burning. She could smell smoke and became alarmed. 'There is a fire! Oh, my God, my God!'

'What is happening?' I asked, suspecting that she was about to re-experience a trauma from the past.

'They are burning *me!*' she called out in horror.

I was not prepared for this, but my training as a Psychosynthesis practitioner enabled me to keep my cool and stick with what was going on for her. 'Why are they burning you? What have you done?' I asked as if these were the most natural questions on Earth.

She was at a loss for a while and felt confused, as she told me afterwards.

I asked again, '*Why* are they burning you?' This seemed to be the key question for her and led to the shocking realization that she was accused of witchcraft, that she was innocent and that she did not deserve to be burned.

'What is happening to you?' I urged her to recall.

'I am tied to a stake. They say I am a witch and they are burning me!' She cried uncontrollably for a while, feeling absolutely petrified.

I encouraged her to fully experience what was happening. This is important. In most situations when a past life spontaneously appears it will be a life in which some tragedy happened. The purpose of the Rebirthing breath is to remove this from the body-memory. The more of the past-life memory is allowed to emerge, the deeper and more complete the cleansing.

'Feel the heat, the fire, the flames,' I said calmly and then, 'allow the flames to purify you.'

After a little while the look on Marcia's face changed from distorted agony to sudden bliss. 'Feel the heat and let it sweep through you,' I said gently. With the numbness now gone she could breathe freely again, more powerfully than before. 'Let the flames consume you,' I said softly. And then, spontaneously, 'Now move forward to the point of death, when your soul leaves your body. Go to the last breath.'

Suddenly Marcia stopped breathing and went limp. All life seemed to have gone from her. I sat and waited. After about four minutes I began to worry. She looked lifeless and her face had lost all colour. Her lips were turning blue. What was I to do? I knew about breath-suspensions, when the client's breathing suddenly stops, and that they were perfectly normal and safe, but nobody had told me how long they were supposed to last. What if she really had died? How would I explain this? 'Breathe,' I told myself. 'Keep calm and stay with the process, this is what is meant to happen.'

Finally, after what seemed like an eternity, Marcia opened her eyes and looked at me warmly. A big smile spread across her face. She took a deep breath and then said without effort, 'Oh, Deike, dying is so beautiful.' She looked absolutely ecstatic.

She closed her eyes and started the rhythmic breathing again. After several more minutes she called out joyfully: 'The light! The light! Brighter than bright, but it does not hurt my eyes.' Her whole body seemed to be breathing and moving rhythmically now. She continued until, as she told me later, 'I was consumed by the light.' She felt as if she had touched upon something sacred, something so good and pure that cleansed her whole being.

Marcia's agoraphobia disappeared after this one session, never to return. Subsequently she had more Rebirths which brought to consciousness further incidences of public exposure and shaming from past lives. The breathing removed all of them from her body-memory soon after they emerged.

Marcia did not show symptoms of public exposure or shaming during our work together, except for a mild fear of examinations. I felt, however, that given her high degree of intelligence and her talent for prose writing, she was not living up to her potential. Behind examination anxiety, however mild, one will frequently find a past-life story of public exposure or persecution for what one 'knows,' frequently leading to a public execution *(see also Part II).*

Had it not been for my knowledge of how to work with bodily symptoms, I doubt whether her past-life trauma could have emerged. I would probably have tried to keep her relaxed and diverted her from going deeper.

When one first encounters a breath-suspension outside a training session, in the privacy of one's own consulting room, it can be alarming. The tendency might be to start the person breathing again by talking to them or touching them. This is a mistake. The breath-suspension will last as long as it does and when it is over the person will always feel warm, light and secure. Remember that you cannot die by holding your breath. When you need to breathe you will start to do so spontaneously. *(See also pages 173–4.)*

Fear of Flying or a Breath of Fresh Air?

Recently I flew from London to Dublin to give a two-day Rebirthing workshop and also to see ten people for individual sessions over a three-day period. This was quite a workload and I had only two days in which to teach the basic theory and practice of Rebirthing. I needed to adjust my teaching material to the requirements of this group and hoped to be able to do this on the plane. I had a lot of files to go through, and I hoped for an empty seat beside me so I could spread out my papers. At the check-in desk the clerk reassured me that if I took a seat at the rear of the airplane there would be plenty of space, but I could see, as I waited at the gate, that this would be a crowded flight.

When I reached my seat I found the other two seats in the row already occupied.

'Are you afraid of flying?' came a voice.

I looked down. A woman in her mid-forties was looking up at me with big frightened eyes.

'No,' I said.

'Well, I am, and I might grab hold of you during the flight. I panic during take-off and landing,' she warned me.

I smiled politely, hoping she would not disturb me during the flight. We sat in silence, each browsing through a newspaper.

When the plane started moving the woman grabbed hold of my arm instinctively, but then let go again. I was surprised that she should so readily let her fear show to a perfect stranger. She covered her face with her hands, bent forward and started rocking and groaning. Her husband, next to her, tried to comfort her, but she crossly pushed his hand away. We were still only taxiing to the runway.

'You should just breathe strongly,' I said to the woman, uncomfortably, as I had no idea how she would receive my advice. 'You cannot concentrate on your breathing *and* be afraid at the same time,' I continued.

I don't think she heard me. Her right hand was pressed hard against her mouth and nose as if to stop herself from breathing altogether. She remained sitting like this while we waited to take off. Then the engines revved and their power began to thrust the plane forward.

'Oh, my God!' she exclaimed, truly panicking now. She tried to grab hold of me again.

'Just breathe,' I said calmly, 'deeply, into the top of your chest.' But she was too tense and frightened to think about breathing. If her seat-belt had not been fastened she would have curled up into a ball.

The next thing I knew I was gently pushing her back into an upright position, taking her hand away from her mouth and putting my right hand on her upper chest. I applied a little pressure and then said quite firmly, not expecting any argument, 'Now, breathe as if you were trying to push my hand up with your inhale.' I think she was too scared to object and started breathing. We had attracted a certain amount of attention from other passengers, but I decided to proceed. All this happened within seconds as the plane was racing along the runway. Then we started to take off.

Again and again the woman tried to cover her nose and mouth with her hand, but I prevented it, encouraging her to breathe in the same way. 'Just concentrate on the breathing!' I repeated several times, as I carefully watched her upper chest. When it stopped moving I put my hand on it again and said: 'Push my hand up!' She was now breathing with more confidence and even smiled at me. 'Good,' I kept encouraging her. 'Keep it up like that.' I pretended that there was nothing to it and started reading again. She kept breathing and slowly began to relax. Then the take-off was completed. 'There,' I said, 'We are up in the air. You've done it!'

I shall never forget the look on her face. She leaned forward, slapped her thighs and said in disbelief, 'That is the easiest take-off I have ever experienced. This breathing really does something. I feel so light. You are a miracle!' She looked radiant, smiling from ear to ear, and was very pleased with herself.

'*You've* done it,' I reminded her. I was very moved by all this and felt that for some reason fate had placed me next to her. She had clearly been in an almost unbearable agony and now she was as relaxed as any of the other passengers.

She asked me more about the breathing, then we talked about her children and her dog. 'I am feeling incredible, happy even,' she said. I was wondering what would happen when we came in to land. Meantime the woman was talking about the wedding she was going to in Ireland and how it was worth making this flight and going through this 'life and death drama' to get there. Her husband kept looking at me as if I was some sort of witch who had cast a spell over his wife. I suppose he couldn't believe that for once they had got through take-off without an embarrassing drama.

Shortly afterwards the captain's voice came over the amplifier informing us that we were preparing to land. The woman continued to chat away about this and that and did not seem to have heard the announcement. But she did take the occasional deep breath, quite naturally. We landed without further ado and she turned to me, beaming, and said, 'This has been the best flight I have ever been on. Thank you so much.' Inside the terminal she thanked me once more and said, 'I will never forget you. I can now look forward to the wedding knowing that I can do the breathing again on the flight back. It is an absolute miracle!'

I know that the breathing had not only distracted her from feeling afraid but had also removed some, perhaps all, of the cause of her fear of flying.

As all phobias are irrational reactions to some unknown cause, trying to 'understand' them is futile. The only thing that really works is removing the cause. Whether we understand the cause or not is not important. But releasing the negative memory, burning it up with the breath, so to speak, is.

When something has been removed from the unconscious mind it ceases to have power over us. It no longer exists. This woman did not tell me what exactly she was experiencing during the flight and I did not ask her. Maybe an ancient fear returned; maybe she fell from a great height in a past life or crashed in an airplane in a previous incarnation.

One woman I Rebirthed, who also had a fear of flying, was afraid that the plane would explode and she would not have enough time to make her peace with God. We only had one session, but it brought to consciousness a deeply seated religious conflict that might reveal traumatic events involving death and torture in past lives.

Near-Death on the Nile

Three years ago Ean and I went to Egypt at the end of January to catch some winter sun and to celebrate my birthday. We spent the first two nights in a hotel by the Red Sea enjoying the white sandy beaches and swimming in the cool, clean waters. On the second morning, at about 4:30, we went on a long bumpy drive, in a beaten-up old Jeep, across a roadless stretch of desert, with four other people: Cecilia, a dark, slim reporter for an English newspaper, her tall, blond and tanned boyfriend, Sam, and a French couple.

The purpose of this self-imposed torture was to see the sun rising. It was the tour guide's suggestion and we went along with it because we never like to miss out on anything, but secretly I was wondering what could be so special about a sunrise. I had seen dozens of them all over the world.

We eventually drove up a very steep hill, so steep that I did not think that we would make it. We came to an abrupt stop at the top. We were told that this was the best spot. The desert was still shrouded in complete darkness. We were early and had another forty minutes to wait. I had no idea that the desert could be so cold at night. Only the two Egyptians, the driver and the guide, were wearing warm coats. A hip-flask of duty-free whisky was passed around. We tried our best to stay cheerful, but the only thing you can do in the desert, when it is pitch black, is to look up at the sky.

And what heavens they turned out to be. There was the slimmest slither of a new crescent moon beside the brightest Venus I have ever seen. There was Mercury a little below Venus, and

Mars up to the left, imposing and seeking attention with his red aura. Jupiter and Saturn, the two ancient giants, stood silently watching. Uranus, Neptune and Pluto were also up there but, obviously, too far away to see with the naked eye.

We all stood there in awe. Even the Egyptians, who go out there regularly, were impressed by the celestial line-up. Ean and I are keen sky-watchers but have never had the privilege of seeing all the planets (except the outer ones of course) in the sky at the same time, and we will probably never again.

Slowly, very slowly, it began to get lighter. Our guide asked us to turn our backs to where the sun was coming from and look in the opposite direction. A dim pink light began to appear. It was a mere suggestion of a rosy hue on the tips of the mountains facing the sun that was still beneath the horizon. We stood for quite a while watching the pink get stronger and brighter and spreading over a larger area.

'Look!' someone shouted. 'The sun!'

We swung round and there, quite suddenly, the sun had appeared, its light pouring over the desert like golden lava. And then came the strange wind that accompanies the rising desert sun.

We all stood there for a long time in wonder at the colors, the fast-rising sun and the celestial line-up spread out overhead in a wondrous web of dotted stars, now joined by the sun and still definitely visible in the crisp, clear sky. Cecilia, clearly overwhelmed by such ancient beauty, was crying, and so was the Frenchman. Eventually, reluctantly, we left to have breakfast of rolls and sweet tea in a desert village with a Bedouin family, before embarking on a camel ride. I was aware for the rest of the day that Cecilia was strangely silent.

The following day again we rose before sunrise and went on a seven-hour journey in a battered and uncomfortable bus, without air-conditioning, to Luxor, where we were going to board a Nile cruise ship. The heat at times seemed unbearable. We felt sticky and thirsty and only stopped twice to stretch our legs. For most of

the way we had a military escort to protect us from possible terror-
ist attacks, which, oddly enough, I found rather exciting. Cecilia,
however, did not take well to the heat and seemed alarmed by the
constant presence of armed vehicles.

We reached Luxor safely and spent the following three nights
on the ship going downriver towards Aswan. We visited several
magnificent temples and other historic sites each day but mostly in
the morning, while it was still cool enough, or after sunset. Much
to Cecilia's dismay this meant rising at five a.m. A few visits were
scheduled for late morning as well. Fortunately, the ship was
equipped with a much-needed swimming-pool for cooling off
before lunch.

On the second day, the hottest day so far, I was just coming out
of the pool when I saw someone lying on a sun lounger in the
shade with several people standing around. I asked what the matter
was. 'She's had an asthma attack,' someone said to me. I looked
down and saw that it was Cecilia. She had told us that she suffered
from asthma and that she used a ventilator, but it did not look like
an asthma attack to me. Her face was grey, her lips were pale, she
was making no effort to breathe and, in fact, seemed to have
stopped breathing altogether. Her body looked completely rigid.

'Is there anything I can do?' I asked.

'Please just keep away. We are nurses and we know how to deal
with this,' a young girl warned me.

Still something prevented me from leaving the scene. Although
Cecilia was dressed in shorts and a T-shirt she looked to me as
though she was freezing cold. Her boyfriend was standing next to
me, clearly worried. 'She is in shock,' I whispered to him, as I did
not want to elicit a negative reaction from the nurses. 'Go and get a
blanket and cover her up.' When he had returned and covered her,
I let him know that I had Arnica with me, a homeopathic anti-
shock remedy I always carry in case of emergencies, and asked him
to see whether she would like some. Cecilia was obviously still
conscious, for she opened her eyes just wide enough to see that it

was me and gave a barely perceptible nod. I raced down to our cabin to fetch the remedy and put the little white glucose tablet under Cecilia's tongue.

I don't know what the nurses made of me but they suddenly disappeared. I placed my hand lightly on Cecilia's upper chest and encouraged her to imagine that she was breathing in through her feet all the way up through her body to where my hand lay. As she was so weak, she could only breathe very lightly. She was still stiff and there was no improvement in the colour of her skin, but at least I had contact with her and she was now breathing rhythmically. After a few minutes she began to relax. I encouraged her to continue to make an effort to breathe in a certain way with the emphasis on the inhale. This was not altogether easy, as she was very weak and kept wanting to just 'slip away.' But every time her breathing weakened I exerted light pressure on her chest and asked her to push it up with her breath.

Eventually, her body began to warm up, colour returned to her cheeks and her breathing became more powerful. After approximately thirty minutes she began to smile. Her face took on an almost angelic look and I could tell that she was approaching the often ecstatic end of a Rebirth. This told me that she had pulled through, that vital life force was circulating through her body and that it would be safe enough to leave her in the care of her boyfriend. I instructed him to keep her breathing a while longer until she felt that she had completed the breathing cycle.

The following day Cecilia, still looking and feeling fragile, told me that a similar incident had happened three years earlier. Then she had been rushed to hospital and put in intensive care and almost died. This time, too, she thought she would die.

She explained: 'After the Arnica tablet I can remember an overwhelming sense of relief at knowing I was not going to die, for that was the overriding feeling until that moment. My strongest memory is of the hour that followed, when you and Sam were either side of me on deck and talking to me and trying to get rid of the rigidity and cold in my feet. I remember you saying that I was having rapid eye movement and that is when I started seeing tombs, Egyptian ones unmistakably, and the long tunnels that led to them. I saw in my mind the paintings on the walls and ceilings. It was pleasant and not frightening. It was only the following day in the Valley of the Kings that I realized I had seen these tombs in my visions on the boat yet I had never visited such a place before. Although I have seen films/documentaries and pictures in books it was a very real vision I experienced and it even smelt and felt like a large tomb.'

Later, when we met again in London she said, 'I could feel and see everything as if it was for real. The breathing helped me through it until, finally, I felt so warm and glowing and simply went into a very bright light. I shall never forget this, it was the most amazing experience I have ever had in my life.'

She did not need to use her ventilator for the rest of the holiday and after a Rebirthing session in London a few weeks after the Egyptian trip the effect on her asthma was dramatic. Now she rarely uses the ventilator and has even been jogging without too much discomfort.

Shortly after her 'breathing session' on the ship in Egypt Cecilia told me that she felt she had been entombed alive and that she could not breathe. This could account for her asthma and the drastic reaction to being in Egypt again, visiting tombs and hearing accounts of embalmments and burials. However, her collapse had not been preceded by an asthma attack.

My own belief is that Cecilia's past-life memory of a life in Egypt that ended in tragedy was triggered from day one of her arrival. The emotions aroused by the sunrise would have stirred her deeply, making her more open to the impressions that were to come in the following few days, but also just being in the place would have triggered images, sounds and bodily sensations that were deeply stored in the cellular system of her body-mind.

The fact that the removal of this memory had such healing results, that Cecilia now only rarely uses a ventilator, goes jogging and has more the kind of life she envisions for herself suggests those memories were creating life-threatening problems.

I am still in touch with Cecilia and each time we meet she mentions how her 'session' was a turning-point. My observation of her session in London was somewhat different from her experience. I just saw her lying there quietly breathing for an hour. Nothing seemed to be happening. She had come with great hopes of an equally powerful experience and I was beginning to think that she might be disappointed when, at last, as I could tell by the pace and depth of her breathing, she reached the end of the breathing cycle and suddenly opened her eyes. 'That was amazing!' she exclaimed, to my surprise. 'Wow, what an experience!'

Later she added, 'I vividly remember going from extreme peace and contentment to a short period where I felt I was crying – I don't know why – and then into an extraordinary phase where I was actually living though a scene in a book I was reading by Umberto Eco. The ship on the front cover had come to life and the island around it – that certainly has never happened before or since!'

Sheena

The following account is taken from the diary of Sheena, a beautiful, gentle woman in her late twenties, who came to me 'just to try it out.' She describes a Rebirthing session during which her first child was conceived:

> On April 21, 1991 I had a Rebirthing session with Deike. I remember it well because it took place on her houseboat on the Thames and because during that session I felt the spirit of my child, who was born on January 15, 1992, enter my body.
>
> The experience began with a deep feeling of darkness and fear. Visualizations came to me of rape, evil and death as I passed through this darkness. I watched from outside my body as I was abused and then, as a free-floating spirit, I was released and said

goodbye to that life of sadness. [She then experienced herself being born in another body.] As I saw myself passing down the birth canal, I was surrounded by orange light. It was like a golden shield rotating, whirling ahead of me. It was the most beautiful colour. Deep feelings of joy penetrated me as I experienced this colour, which came inside me as a glowing light. I felt beautiful. I wanted to wear lavish colors, to dance and sing. When I came out of the breathing session, I felt born anew and I also felt that new life abounded within me.

When I returned home, my husband, Jeremy, could not express how well and glowing I looked. A few days later we did a pregnancy test and it was positive. Jeremy said then that he knew I was pregnant the moment I left Deike's boat! Certainly, the spirit of my child, Jasmine, seemed to enter my body on that day, even if the physical creation had occurred earlier.

Sheena continued Rebirthing each month until her child was born. The birth was easy and trouble-free and all those present were ecstatic when they witnessed the arrival of robust, pink and bursting-with-energy Jasmine.

I have learned over the years to trust the process of Rebirthing and not to attempt to control it. Our psyches are much wiser than our conscious minds. If we step aside, get out of our own way, something can indeed happen, and most of the time this is totally unexpected and life-changing and exactly what needs to happen next.

 THE MAGIC OF
THE BREATH

Breathe the air with love, and reflect that God is within it.
Deep breathing is the conscious appreciation of air and the
love of the vital forces that it contains. Air is an expression of
the Love of the Great Cosmic Powers that are the source of all
visible manifestations.
Beinsa Douno (1864–1944)

[The real purpose of prolonged singing and chanting] is to
increase the concentration of CO_2 in the lungs and blood and so
lower the efficiency of the cerebral reducing valve, until it will
admit biologically useless material from Mind-at-Large.
Aldous Huxley

Why should it be that breathing in and out in a certain rhythmical
manner has such a profound effect on our souls and minds?
Breathing in is like inhaling food for the soul. We breathe in divine
substance from the invisible and, with it, when we breathe out,
we are bringing something else into manifestation. So, through

extracting life force from the air and exhaling transformed matter we are actually bringing spirit into matter.

Paying attention to the breath means holding the key to enlightenment. That is why breathing, chanting and the rhythmic repetition of mantras are considered of such vital importance in many religious practices. By concentrating on rhythmical breathing, the soul enters a meditative state and the mind becomes calm and empty. When the mind is empty it can make contact with the universal mind.

In Chinese medicine the lungs are the dwelling-place of the soul and the root of *Qi* (*prana* or vital life force), which is considered the sum total of Mind, Spirit and Life.

To the ancient Greeks 'breath' and 'spirit' were the same word, as they also are in many other languages. We cannot separate the one from the other. Spirit is all around us and breathing is our main connection to it.

Therefore, it would stand to reason that the better and more powerfully and rhythmically we breathe, the more contact we can make with the spiritual side of life. Spirit comes in on the breath to the lungs, from where respiration is administered to the entire body. Without breath no life inside a human being would be possible. Breathing connects us to universal forces that have the power to cleanse and heal our bodies and minds and to widen our consciousness.

Because we breathe all day long, mostly unconsciously, we don't give much thought to what we are actually doing. It is only when something goes wrong, when our breathing becomes restricted through ill health or suffocation, that fresh air becomes the most precious thing on Earth. Yet breathing is perhaps the most mysterious of all the bodily functions. During its uterine life a baby receives its oxygen from the mother whilst at the same time growing a beautiful pair of lungs. When it is born it starts to breathe independently and with that first breath starts its individual journey through life. But what exactly it is, apart from air, that comes into our bodies on the breath has not yet been fully explored and investigated – certainly not by science. Scientists can tell us what happens to our bodies if we increase our breathing speed or if we hold our breath until we almost pass out, but they cannot tell us what specific properties of the breath have the ability to heal diseases of mind and body. Science cannot tell us what spirit, in the sense of divine energy, actually is.

We do know that we need oxygen to survive and that filling our lungs with fresh air is good for us. We also know that the heart pumps good clean blood into the body and that the venous blood, returning to the heart, is laden with waste matter. The more efficiently and more powerfully that we breathe, therefore, the more waste matter will be expelled from our bodies.

I was most astonished when I learned that only 3 percent of body waste is expelled through defecation and only a further 7 percent through urination. Most of us are brought up to believe that emptying our bowels in the morning is vital to our well-being and that if you do not do so you will have problems during the day. This is not to say that this function is not essential for bodily well-being, far from it, but correct breathing is even more important.

A further 20 percent of body waste is discharged through the skin. Again, I found this fact astonishing. As children, when my sisters or I had a temperature, our mother would give us a tepid wash down and put us back to bed with a warm drink, thus allowing the body to deal with the cause of the fever naturally. So I learned early that the skin is important in regulating the body's temperature system, health and vitality, especially during illness, but I had no idea, until I saw these figures, that our skin works for us day and night in order to keep us clean internally. We are told that body-brushing is good for us but we are only seldom given the facts of what happens when we stimulate our skin in this manner. When you realize that body-brushing not only removes dead skin but also opens pores and increases blood-flow to the surface of the skin, thus assisting the body's cleansing process, it takes on a different meaning.

But by far the greatest surprise to me was the fact that as much as 70 percent of bodily waste matter is *breathed out*. This knowledge alone has had the strongest effect on the way I now breathe. Just think about it for a minute. We breathe, mostly unconsciously, all day long, cleansing and purifying our bodies, except that we usually breathe so shallowly, so timidly and without power and enthusiasm, often holding our breath between inhale and exhale, that we spend more time *not* breathing than breathing.

One of the first things many of us do when shocked or frightened is to *hold* our breath. This effectively stops the flow of life force. When in a frightening situation we remember to 'take a deep breath' we are able to support ourselves with the aid of the very same life force that we have previously blocked. Ideally, our habitual breathing pattern should be rhythmical and continuous, without pause.

Exercise is of course a great help in getting us to breathe fully and deeply, but we usually only engage in it for a limited period of time, returning to our inefficient way of breathing as soon as we stop.

Most people breathe just enough to stay alive but no more. Everywhere we can observe bent backs and hunched shoulders. These are only too frequently caused by wrong breathing. Lungs that are squashed and contracted cannot possibly operate at full capacity. Their potential sadly and tragically under-used, they do not supply the blood with enough oxygen to efficiently remove impurities from it. As a result we are not as revitalized by breathing as we could be, our bodies are not fully cleansed of metabolic waste and a state of chronic toxicity is created. This is the cause of much ill health, low energy, poor concentration, irritability and depression. A healthy body and healthy mind go together. When we breathe correctly we cleanse the whole body, including our brain cells. Breathing purifies thoughts and thus changes our minds.

Learning to breathe the Rebirthing breath will not only purify your body and mind and remove all that hinders the flow of life-energy, but it is also the best beauty treatment I know of. As it cleanses your body of impurities it will brighten your eyes and bring a lovely glow to your face as well as smooth out your skin. One of my clients, a woman in her early fifties, who went straight off to a lunch party with girlfriends after a session, was greeted with: 'Goodness, you look as if you've had your face ironed!'

THE STRESS BUSTER

Rebirthing is a powerful technique for releasing stress. People frequently arrive for a session extremely tired, tense, irritable and in need of a rest. Yet after an hour or so of correct breathing the tiredness is gone, the tension has disappeared, and they feel calm and balanced.

Denise, a journalist in her mid-twenties, had an extremely demanding position. She worked late hours on the news-desk most of the time, whenever she was not travelling around the world reporting. She was too busy for a relationship, friends or parties. Her life was summed up in one word: work. She came to see me because she felt stuck in this seemingly never-ending cycle and wondered whether Rebirthing might move her forward.

She was an easy breather and had no difficulty breathing quietly for a whole hour. Nothing much happened; in fact the session appeared to be totally uneventful and almost boring. Later, though, after the session, when she was sitting up with a warm drink, Denise smiled and said, 'My head is so clear, it is indescribable. This is what I have always wanted. I was so afraid that I was going mad because I couldn't switch off my mind.'

Her brain was simply overloaded and she was in danger of suffering burn out. The breathing had cleansed and reordered the workings of her mind and brain and she decided there and then to reorganize her life, to work less and make space in which to be more creative and to see her friends. Shortly after this session she moved from London to the country.

My own theory is that the breathing not only regenerates the cellular structure but also removes harmful factors – like stress-producing memory fragments – from our overloaded daily lives.

THE STORY BEHIND THE STORY

The healthy glow of people who regularly breathe in this way is but a bonus. What is more profoundly important is the astonishing results that can be achieved with conscious connected breathing on unconscious psychic and physical levels.

What surfaces during a session often has no apparent relationship to the reason why people feel they need therapy. There is a story behind the story, a deeper reason behind what is apparently troubling an individual. This is usually buried within the body's cellular structure and is seldom reached by talking.

I have given various examples throughout this book where what emerges during a session is a total surprise and often also completely unknown to the client (i.e. not a memory from this lifetime) and yet is curiously relevant to the present life situation.

My Psychosynthesis training in London included an excellent course in Gestalt therapy conducted by the American couple George and Judith Brown. 'Don't believe the story!' they reminded us constantly. What they meant was, yes, listen to what a client has to say, but do not believe that the reason they are so unhappy, blocked or depressed is because of what they are telling you. We were taught that the real reasons for the difficulties we experience are buried deep within the body-mind memory, as any successful or completed Gestalt will demonstrate. (*Gestalt* is the German word for a complete figure or form. In Gestalt therapy the word is used for a successfully completed piece of work on a problem, when an integration of mind, emotions and body has taken place and previously blocked energy has become available for creative living.) It is my experience that all emotional and mental problems, as well as most physical difficulties, can be traced to blockages in the body's energy system, which, when released, lose their power and influence, as the following example will illustrate.

Ingrid

Ingrid, an attractive, cultured woman in her late fifties came for therapy because she was desperately unhappy. She could see no solution to her misery and felt that life was not worth living. She had a variety of physical symptoms, ranging from food allergies to murderous migraines, cold extremities and chronic congestion and pain in her abdomen, on which she had had several serious operations. We spent a couple of hours examining her past and present, but I couldn't see how talking about her problems would help.

I felt that Ingrid quickly needed to find a different perspective on her whole life. Although she did not quite seem the type who would lie down on the mattress and start doing deep breathing work, I nevertheless suggested Rebirthing therapy to her. She was suspicious at first, but as she was frequently in pain from a stiff neck and the migraines she was prepared to try anything for relief.

Ingrid is a natural breather, that is to say she could breathe correctly from the start, and within minutes powerful energy had begun to course through her body. Material was soon surfacing from the unconscious, manifesting as physical symptoms of stiffness, coldness and tightness. She was not hyperventilating, so I knew that this was not a case of over-breathing. Then her hands, legs and abdomen felt to her as if they had become filled with electricity. Her head became extremely painful and she was very frightened that she might get 'stuck,' that she would 'never get out of this.' What 'this' was she could not tell me, but she knew she felt in great danger. She was experiencing an almost unbearable pressure behind her head. She could not understand what was happening to her. This is a common occurrence and is most often a sign that the person is re-experiencing their actual birth, hence the pressure and fear of getting stuck.

What happened to Ingrid next is not unusual. No great stories emerged, no past lives and no traumas from early childhood. She experienced everything purely on the physical level. There was especial emphasis on the head and abdomen, her two most vulnerable areas. They became so tense and painful that she finally found the whole experience totally unbearable. Her whole body felt in extreme discomfort. By this time she had been breathing for approximately an hour and I felt that we would not get any further this time. I suggested that she returned to normal breathing.

What happened then surprised us both. Within a few minutes she could feel a powerful energy begin to move from her feet upward through the whole of her body, softening and releasing one pain, one blockage after the other until she was perfectly quiet and bathing in a contented warm glow. I then suggested that she turn on her side and went off to make her a hot drink.

When I returned I noticed that she had been crying and gently asked her about it. What had happened was that something long forgotten had returned to consciousness and so could now be released. This was the realization that she had not been present when her father had died and she felt that she should have been there. At this point she was still feeling guilty about it and started crying again. I just stayed with her and let her grieve.

Suddenly she exclaimed, 'Oh, this tea is delicious!' Her face lit up and she started to smile. 'That was amazing!' She felt her tummy, which was now soft and relaxed, then moved her neck from side to side. All her pain had totally disappeared. She looked happy and radiant and wonderful.

Ingrid continued with more sessions, which again mainly affected her physically. We breathed through the operations she had had on her abdomen until she felt that all the cuts and scars had healed. She also re-experienced an operation she had had on the front of her neck a few years earlier, during which it had been wrenched back and damaged. She had completely forgotten about the operation but after this particular Rebirth she knew that it had been the cause of her migraines. Since then she has only had the occasional, much milder, migraine, and that only when she has been under great pressure at work.

Her relationship with her husband, too, has improved a great deal. They have had a couple of holidays which Ingrid described as 'the best time ever together.' She could not think of anything that she had particularly done to change things. But she noticed that she was more relaxed and laid back about life in general.

At the beginning of the therapy I had empathized with Ingrid's situation. I could see clearly that she was suffering, both physically and emotionally. She was having a rotten time and she was working much too hard. But had we tried to solve her problems by talking *about* them, by changing her life from the outside, or by changing her thinking, we might have had some limited success, but the fundamental pathology would still have persisted, as it would have remained untouched. The problems were on the physical body-memory level, a level that cannot be reached through talking about the symptoms that an imbalance or energy blockage there will produce. The magic energy that can enter our bodies with certain types of breathing can, however, release the deepest, densest blocks within our physical as well as subtle bodies.

The unconscious guilt that Ingrid had felt for many years about her absence from her father's deathbed had festered and become an 'energy cyst.' This had no doubt contributed to her general state of tension and lack of self-worth. The multiple operations on her abdomen had stopped the life force from flowing freely through her, causing congestion in that area and interference with circulation, hence her cold hands and feet. During one of her Rebirthing sessions, though, Ingrid felt her physical scars healing. She breathed through them until she felt her muscles and flesh restored completely and her abdomen in a total state of relaxation.

Ingrid is continuing to prosper, living a far more creative life now. Her relationships are flourishing too. We never tried to improve her life – instead we simply allowed the breath to do its healing work. All the obstacles that were preventing the creative life force from reaching and energizing her authentic Self had to dissolve in order for the divine energy of the breath to help her find her right direction and life purpose.

Irritable Bowel Syndrome, Phobias and Cigarettes

One physical complaint that can be rapidly relieved by breathing is irritable bowel syndrome, which more and more people, especially women, seem to be suffering from these days.

Karen, who is in her late forties, sought help from Rebirthing specifically for the abdominal pains, cramps, bloatedness and chronic constipation she had suffered for two years. During her session she found herself back in a past life as a man on safari in Africa hunting white rhino with two other men. When the rhino came into full view the man stood transfixed admiring the beautiful beast but was unable to shoot it. At this point he knew that he would be killed by the rhino, but he just sobbed, 'It's so beautiful, I cannot shoot!' He was aware that he was making a conscious choice to die rather than kill this rare animal. The rhino charged and buried its horn in the man's lower left side and killed him. The horn went in at the exact place where Karen had been experiencing the greatest discomfort: her descending colon. Her painful symptoms and constipation disappeared magically the same day. She also later realized that this experience had given her a penetrating insight into the part of herself that feels deeply connected to nature.

Aldous Huxley, in *Heaven and Hell*, talks at length about the 'preternatural significance' that people find in altered-state experiences. His experiences were drug-induced and not accompanied by the physical cleansing and regeneration that are the God-given gift of the breath, however the insights that some people gain from rhythmic breathing sound very similar. It would appear, then, that changes in brain chemistry take place during Rebirthing that resemble those induced by some hallucinogenic drugs.

Why did Karen carry this particular memory in her colon, producing such painful symptoms? Was it the old wound inflicted by the white rhinoceros or was it guilt about having been a hunter? The main point here is that the breath can reach certain parts of our bodies that carry very specific memories which cause physical problems (as well as mental ones) for as long as they remain festering away in the unconscious body-mind system.

The case of Antony, a dynamic business executive, shows how mental anguish can also be relieved by breathing in a certain rhythmic manner. Antony suffered from all kinds of fears – fear of crossing bridges (he had to cross a bridge over the River Thames each time he came to see me), of being in high places, of being underground, of flying and of eating in restaurants. He booked in for ten weekly sessions. No past-life scenarios emerged and no early childhood memories that might have provided a trigger for his phobias. He sweated profusely during the first couple of breathing sessions, but had no associations to this. But each time he had a session he became calmer and calmer until none of the phobias remained. He recently wrote to me, a year after his last session: 'I have felt increasingly better as time has gone on, so I wonder whether Rebirthing has longer term benefits that have yet to be appreciated?'

Although Rebirthing is a reliable method of treating successfully many types of fears and phobias I have always found it extremely difficult to work with people who are on strong medication for these conditions. The first thing that breathing will cleanse out of the body will be the poisonous residues from the drugs. The client will feel much better at the end of each session, more optimistic and better able to plan for the future, but by the next session we are back to square one. For people who are on medication for anxiety and/or depression it would be advisable to reduce the dosage, with their doctor's help, whilst at the same time undergoing a course of Rebirthing therapy.

Simon was sent to me by his psychiatrist. He was on two different types of very strong drugs to control his depression, agitation and sleeplessness. He was also smoking forty cigarettes a day. He had tried to commit suicide several times and assured me that he still thought of doing so every day. I knew I had a terrific challenge here in trying to break through this cycle of drug-taking and smoking.

Moreover, Simon was a reluctant breather. He couldn't understand why he needed to take in more breath than usual, although I had already explained the mechanics of conscious connected breathing. He kept opening his eyes during the session, asking whether this would do him any good. After a few minutes of breathing he would start to release the tar and/or nicotine of the last cigarette he had just smoked, which, of course, stimulated in him the desire to have another one. So he would try and get up to have a cigarette there and then.

We never got very far, although Simon was calmer and more relaxed at the end of each of the two sessions he had with me. He did not continue because he was unwilling to reduce his drug dosage (I had suggested that he discuss this with his doctor as he was on far too high a dosage of librium). Unfortunately, he could not take that next step. He did, however, remark after his first session that it was a lovely sunny day and that he would call his girlfriend to take a walk with her. After the final session he was lamenting that he could not have a better relationship with her, that he took her for granted and that she deserved better, as she had stood by him through his illness. His final words to me were: 'Well, I guess I could always try and improve the way I am with her. I have put her through so much.' This remorse sounded genuine and it was the first time that I had heard him take responsibility for his behavior. But I am not optimistic about his prognosis.

I have Rebirthed one young man who was a cocaine addict. After three sessions he kicked the habit and went away to work on a ship. But unless a person sincerely wishes to give up drugs, Rebirthing in itself is of little use, unless the sessions can strengthen the resolve that is already present. I would generally always advise such a person to join Narcotics Anonymous.

THE WILL IN THE BREATH

The breath – or rather the power of the breath – curiously has a will of its own. It is stronger than any resistance we might put up, stronger than any deep-seated fears or prejudices. If you breathe the correct way for long enough you will have a Rebirth, a breakthrough, a spiritual renewal and emergence. The 'spirit-breath,' as it is also called, once activated, will find its own direction through the body and go to the exact place where it is needed. I do not need to work out a 'treatment' plan for any particular client, the spirit-breath knows what it needs to do next, and it is always a surprise.

In my experience, the breath has never brought up and released anything that was already consciously known to the person. As with dreams, which only tell us things that we do not already know, so also with Rebirthing. Yet, at the same time, when a memory returns from our inner underworld we usually recognize it immediately as something that has always been known to us.

I first met this when Kate came for breathing sessions. She had been sent by her dentist as she kept grinding her teeth at night so badly that she was suffering from severe headaches and had to wear a pad between her teeth for protection.

Within minutes of starting to breathe she developed an agonizing headache. It was so bad that she screamed and rolled about on the floor. I had the suspicion that we were tapping into a past life and asked her what was happening and where she was. 'Where I always am. In my bedroom. It is night-time and I am alone. I am six years old and I have this awful headache!' she said angrily through gritted teeth. She was in genuine pain and quite hysterical by now. As she held her swaying head tightly she moaned, 'They have all gone out and left me alone. I have lockjaw and I am about to die!'

I sat quietly encouraging her to stay with what was happening, trusting that the breathing would take her to the next stage quite naturally. Her agony continued a while longer and then she suddenly stopped breathing and lay there lifeless. She seemed to have died. I waited patiently until she resumed breathing. By now I had seen these 'death scenes' often enough not to worry about them. After approximately three or four minutes Kate started to breathe again. She appeared relaxed and I could see by the movement of her eyes behind her closed eyelids that she was observing some inner vision. She was smiling and looked as if she was seeing something extremely beautiful.

When the session was over and she was sipping her hot drink, she told me that she had seen a very bright light. This light, which had begun as a tiny glowing spot in pitch darkness, had grown in intensity and size until she had eventually merged with it. This had happened without any active intent on her part. Out of the light a benevolent presence had gradually emerged, a person emanating immense love and kindness. By this time Kate had felt herself to be in a blissful field, totally at one with all there is, completely at peace and still. This was, she confided, the most amazing spiritual and uplifting experience she had ever had. She also told me that although during the session she knew the final scene of what she called 'that life' very well and that it seemed like a familiar memory that had haunted her for as long as she could remember, this was actually the first time she had become consciously aware of it.

After this session the condition of Kate's jaw improved considerably and so did her life, both personally and professionally.

Although it may appear that the relevant scenarios simply roll out of a person's body-memory during a session – and in a sense that is true – the way they are facilitated is of vital importance. What the facilitator says and how they say it makes all the difference to whether an old memory is triggered or not. In actual practice the process always unfolds gently and gradually, with the Rebirther acting mainly as a guide, reassuring the client and affirming that whatever may be happening at any particular moment during the session is exactly right. As guides, we remind the client, as Huxley put it in *The Doors of Perception*, that 'our goal is to discover that we have always been where we ought to be' and that 'it is faith, or loving confidence, which guarantees that visionary experiences shall be blissful.'

Quite a different situation arose for Elsa, an attractive, highly educated woman in her mid-forties. She was extremely puzzled by what happened to her and so was I. During her first session she started to go into what I can only describe as an epileptic fit but without the foaming at the mouth and grinding of teeth or biting of the tongue. She was not particularly disturbed by this, although she felt very uncomfortable. The fit lasted for a few minutes, then gradually subsided and changed into a dance movement which she demonstrated with her arms and hands. We had no idea what this was about and we both thought the whole thing quite funny and laughed a lot about it afterwards. At the end of the session she felt energized whilst at the same time calm, relaxed and 'almost' happy.

An explanation of this bizarre scenario came the following week when Elsa told me that she had totally forgotten that about ten years earlier she had been given electric shock treatment for depression. It never ceases to amaze me just how accurately the body records experiences, especially traumatizing experiences, even when we are unconscious. The empirical evidence gathered from my work, and that of others who work in similar ways, seems to suggest that most people are in parts, at this deep level, a living Hammer House of Horror, haunted and tortured by events that happened many years, even lifetimes ago, and that refuse to be detected or discovered by analytical or intellectual probing. When these memories begin to be released through rhythmic connected breathing there is always an improvement in the life situation.

It is disturbing to think that most people live apparently reasonably good lives with memories of horrific incidences recorded by, and lodged deep within, their body-memory. How does this affect the people whose lives they touch? How far does it block or delay the emergence of an authentic Self? How does it influence collective behavior and development? There are many more questions one could ask regarding the storage of memories, and their effects, of all types of disasters, atrocities and injustices on individual and/or collective psyches and bodies. In the meantime I shall maintain my motto that these memories are 'better out than in.'

THE BREATH AND BREATHING PROBLEMS

People with all kinds of breathing problems seek help from Rebirthing. In my own experience, however, no one has so far needed to use a ventilator during a session and breathing is always freer and stronger and the chest experienced as wider and fuller.

Once an eleven-year-old boy, Jack, was brought to me by his mother all the way from South America. He was bright, intelligent and charming, but had some kind of non-specific learning difficulty. His birth had been traumatic and he had been delivered with the aid of forceps. The first thing I noticed was that he suffered from severe nasal catarrh which made breathing and talking difficult. He was constantly having to clear his nose and according to his mother he used up at least four man-sized handkerchiefs each day. He interrupted our first session dozens of times because of breathing difficulties and to clear his nose. His was the worst case of nasal congestion I had ever come across. His mother told me that he had suffered from this condition since he was very small and that no one expected it ever to disappear.

Fortunately, Jack was able to come to me three times a week until he had had his ten sessions. On each occasion his breathing improved and he needed fewer interruptions to blow his nose until, finally, he stopped producing excess mucus. By the time he returned home his head was completely clear.

Why and how the breathing cleared Jack's sinuses I do not know. It may be that his head was crushed a little by the forceps delivery or that his body was over-producing mucus for some psychosomatic reason. What is certain is that the change in his breathing brought about a change in his body and mind – you might say it 'changed his mind' – and he left a calmer and healthier child.

Even if there are no breathing difficulties, this type of breathing will expand the air passages, increase lung space, widen the throat and higher or lower the resonance of the voice, whichever is appropriate. Heavy smokers feel clean after breathing and people who have had a chesty congestion following a bout of influenza or similar, report a rapid return to health after only one session. After a few sessions *everyone* is able to breathe more deeply and with greater facility. Since we receive life force with our breath it stands to reason that this type of breathing increases vitality and a sense of well-being. And as this extra energy demands to be manifested in some type of activity – since it cannot just exist in a vacuum but seeks to move around – as a result we find ourselves more active, capable and willing to create the life that is right for us.

I have stopped trying to analyze exactly why people's lives change so rapidly with Rebirthing breathing. I only know that I can fully trust the breath to act as a healing force in whatever way is necessary. For me it is enough that the incoming spiritual energy works as a great alchemical force, transforming base matter into gold.

 BIRTH

When the time comes for the embryo
to receive the spirit of life
at that time the sun begins to help.
This embryo is brought into movement,
for the sun quickens it with spirit.

Rumi

Birth is the first and most important event in your life here on
Earth. It is an archetypal event of manifestation as an individual
and independent human being. How you were born, the type of
experience you had inside the womb and the type of welcome you
received when you arrived are of the utmost importance and can
profoundly influence your subsequent physical, emotional, mental
and spiritual development and well-being.

AWARENESS IN THE WOMB

By the time you are born you have been living for approximately nine months inside a womb, in a liquid environment, warm and protected, surrounded by muffled sounds and comforted by your mother's heartbeat. For the majority of people this time is one of *mystical participation* – you and your mother are as one. No demands are made upon you. You are nourished through the umbilical cord and even your breathing is done for you.

Although attempts are being made to find out what foetuses and babies know and remember, only a small amount of information is beginning to emerge. We know from intrauterine photography that embryos can amuse themselves. They will suck their thumbs, for instance, or play with the cord. Researchers have also discovered that babies can remember music played to them when their mothers were only twenty weeks pregnant, four weeks earlier than previously assumed. Of course, they may eventually determine that the foetus registers and remembers sounds earlier still.

Although a foetus's reasoning abilities and brain memory are not yet fully developed, we now know from Rebirthing and other types of bodywork therapy that facilitate the release of body-memory, as well as from hypnosis, that all these intrauterine experiences are nevertheless stored somewhere in its being. It would appear that the physical brain is not the only place where memory can be stored. So, you will have recorded your whole journey from conception to birth, in detail. All your emotions will be there, your fears and aspirations. You may well ask at this point: 'How do we know this?' If people can remember their birth in very great detail and can also remember past lives, as borne out by Rebirthing, then there is no reason to believe that not *all* past experiences are stored. Medical research into the functions of the brain has shown that stimulating certain areas of the brain (points on the temporal lobes) will bring back long-forgotten memories, some from early childhood, including nursery rhymes and songs.

What is more, you can even have an indication of the kind of life that lies ahead. Some people, including myself, had a clear vision of the life ahead whilst still in the womb. On more than one occasion, someone has refused to be born. It can also take a few sessions before someone feels truly incarnated and committed to their present life, i.e. accepts that they have in some obscure way *chosen* to be here.

We are also slowly acquiring data relating to the awareness of pain and stress in both foetus and baby. In January 1997, Hélène Feger, health correspondent for Britain's *Sunday Express*, cited pioneering British research carried out at the famous Queen Charlotte Maternity Hospital in London. The findings state that babies may be suffering as much pain and stress during childbirth as their mothers. As the newspaper article also pointed out, 'Until twenty years ago doctors were taught that babies did not feel pain and major operations, including heart surgery, were performed [on them] without anaesthesia.'

Dr Vivette Glover of the above hospital said: 'It is surprising that terrific attention is paid to pain relief for the mother during birth, but no attention is currently paid to whether the baby is feeling any pain.' Glover feels that this aspect of obstetrics is hardly being discussed in spite of the fact that some types of deliveries, especially when suction or forceps are used, could be 'extremely painful to the baby.' She agrees with what Rebirthers have discovered in their work with clients – that babies born by forceps delivery can be extremely bruised and that the use of suction can elongate the head. 'It is very likely that this is stressful or painful for the baby,' she comments. The hospital's research showed that foetuses undergoing certain treatment procedures registered an increase of as much as 600 percent in the stress hormones cortisol and the beta-endorphins. Premature babies also showed an increase of ten times higher than normal.

A more recent article in the *Daily Mail* (February 19, 1998), by David Derbyshire, science correspondent in Philadelphia, reports

Dr Michael Commons of Harvard Medical School in Boston as stating that 'High levels of cortisol [in babies] increase the chances of mental illnesses and post-traumatic stress disorder in later life' and that 'Babies are particularly vulnerable to stress chemicals during the first seven months.'

In 1966, the year of my first daughter's birth, many doctors did not believe that babies could feel pain or stress and the common practice was still at times to pull a newborn baby up by its feet, jerking the spine into a straight line (which in itself must have been agonizing for the baby) and slapping its bottom. (I was happy to hear recently from Euan Laird, consultant obstetrician at the Horton Hospital in Banbury, Oxfordshire, that he has personally never seen this.) In 1966, though, they were still separating babies from mothers for several hours at a time, only bringing the newborn in when the *nurse* thought it needed feeding. In fact, it was thought harmful to breastfeed the infant for the first two days. The poor things had to be content with sweetened water until then.

Now whether foetuses, premature babies and newborns feel pain or stress has become such a hot issue that even politicians in Britain have become involved in the debate. British Liberal MP David Alton is concerned that evidence about fetal pain is being suppressed. In an article in the *Sunday Express* (January 1997), he says that we have laws that protect animal foetuses from any scientific procedure that might inflict pain on them, but we do not have the same protection for human foetuses in the womb. At the time this article appeared, doctors were still divided about the use of pain relief for the foetus before performing operations inside the womb.

But even as recently as 1998 an 'expert' on pain from the Manchester Hope Hospital, Dr Stuart Derbyshire, was quoted in the *Sunday Express* (January 28, 1998) as saying: 'Pain is a learned process. For a foetus or baby to feel pain it has to be able to *understand* [my italics] what is going on. A foetus or newborn child is not able to do that.' I wonder how he knows this. Any mother could tell him otherwise.

Just how little attention doctors used to pay to the baby's condition, pain and stress was demonstrated by Mary, a nun, now in her sixties. Her mother developed life-threatening difficulties during a long and painful labor and according to the doctor Mary was born dead. She appeared lifeless and did not breathe. The doctor put her aside on a pile of newspapers to dispose of her later. He then attended to the mother. When she was settled he prepared to dispose of Mary's body, but as he picked her up she started crying, making wonderfully loud sounds with a hitherto unused pair of powerful lungs! One cannot imagine what this newborn was experiencing while she was lying there, cold, rejected and left for dead.

When my own second daughter was born in 1971 things had not improved much in terms of recognizing infant distress. Pregnancy and labor went smoothly, contractions started at five o'clock in the morning and Anna was born four hours later. In fact the midwife did not realize how close I was to giving birth because I was not screaming. As it was she had no time in the end to get me ready. Anna arrived when *she* wanted to and without much difficulty.

They took her away straightaway, without even showing her to me, to 'clean her up.' I was then told that I had a small tear and that they had telephoned my doctor, who lived a few miles away, to come and sew me up. The doctor finally arrived four hours after I had given birth and after he had finished his morning surgery. All this time I was left lying in the delivery room whilst Anna was somewhere else in the building. They would not bring her to me until the doctor had tended to me, after which I was finally wheeled into a large, empty, freezing cold ward. There was still no sign of my daughter. Eventually I demanded that the nurse bring me my child at once. When she returned with the small screaming bundle she said grumpily, 'I could have smashed her head against the side of the bath, she screamed so much,' dumped her unceremoniously on my bed and left. Yes, Anna was screaming alright. I opened my nightgown and put her to my breast. She stopped crying immediately and started to suckle.

A short time later Anna's father arrived and I asked him to take me home there and then as I found the hostile atmosphere of the hospital unbearable. A couple of hours later I was sitting up in my own warm bed, sipping champagne, with Anna contentedly tucked into my side. I placed a tiny drop of champagne on her lips. She seemed to lap it up with great relish. We both slept well that night.

Throughout her childhood and well into her teens, however, Anna suffered from separation anxiety. She would not spend a single night away from home, unless she was with a member of her family. She missed out on all holidays other than family ones. After a few Rebirthing sessions, she finally lost this fear. The fact that I was there in person each time she finished Rebirth might have helped.

BIRTH

For most babies birth is a trauma, even if all goes well and the birth is a relatively easy one. The size of the baby plays a large part in the type of delivery one can expect. If forceps have to be used then obviously the birth will be more traumatic. But the shift from a liquid to an atmospheric environment is in itself stressful enough. Nowadays many women choose to give birth in a pool of water to ease this transition as much as possible. But other stressful events occur before then.

After nine relatively quiet months inside the womb, there is the sudden disturbance of contractions. You probably experienced this as the first rumblings of an earthquake. Then they get stronger. Gradually you are pushed and squeezed further and further down towards the birth canal, the end of which is still shut. You feel trapped. You cannot go back and you cannot go forward. You are well and truly stuck. For some babies this predicament can last many hours, days even, whilst others slip through it with remarkable speed. Most spend sufficient time in this position to be concerned, if not downright panic-stricken, wondering whether they will ever get out.

Finally there is an opening but it is narrow, too narrow. How will the head get through? Isn't it far too big? Well, yes, it is, but nature has devised a most remarkable way in which mother and baby can co-operate with one another during this perilous transition. I am indebted to Euan Laird, for the following information. The pelvis relaxes and 'softens' and the opening can widen. What is more, the soft tissues of the skull undergo what is known as *caput*, which means that the head is squeezed. There is room for movement in the sutures and fontanelle (the membranous space in the infant's skull) and this will allow fetal skull moulding, enabling the two plates of the head to override, thus reducing the width of the head and allowing the baby to push through with greater ease and the least discomfort, if conditions are ideal.

But by now, after being trapped, perhaps for hours, the infant can be quite stressed, and at the same time it is still being pushed forward. Its head feels as if it is being crushed and the baby has no idea what is happening or where it is going. As far as it is concerned this is the end and it will not survive.

Birth Patterns

There probably is no such thing as a perfect birth. Most of us carry unpleasant memories from our birth and feel uneasy about sudden major life changes as a result. We procrastinate when we need to leave a situation that has become too painful, too boring or in some way has served its purpose. We should move on, yet we feel unable to for one reason or another.

Why is it that we put up with circumstances that are no longer useful and that are even harmful to us? The reason for this most often is fear, especially fear of change, which is frequently associated with fear of loneliness, poverty, abandonment or separation. Essentially it is fear of the unknown that prevents us from moving enthusiastically on to the next stage of life.

The way you were born very much influences how you deal with changes, both big and small. If your birth was a fast one you expect changes to happen quickly. If they don't, you don't believe that they are meant to happen at all and you give up without persisting for any length of time.

Anna's relatively trouble-free and fast birth ensured that when she wants to do something she will just get on with it, and she will choose the shortest, most efficient route to do so. Ean, my husband, and I also had fast births, so we both like things to *move* once we have made a decision. His birth was faster than mine – it only took two-and-half hours. His mother was in the middle of a game of bridge when she excused herself, went upstairs to her four-poster bed and gave birth without any fuss. She had been having contractions for the past two hours, but as this was her fourth child she wasn't particularly concerned, told no one, as she did not want to spoil the game, and quietly continued playing her hand. Ean still expects things to happen quickly, without fuss and with the greatest of ease – and of course they do, most of the time.

My birth only took about four hours, but I was born in the middle of winter (Ean was born in the summer) and there was a war on. Whilst Ean's mother only had to interrupt her bridge game and disappear upstairs, mine, having been evacuated to the country to escape heavy bombing, was living in a couple of cold rooms on a farm with my three sisters. When I signalled my arrival she had to quickly organize a baby-sitter and transport to the nearest hospital. Whilst Ean's mother had her husband by her side, my father was on a ship on the other side of the world.

It is not only a question of fast or slow birth, then, but also of the circumstances surrounding that birth. Although Ean and I don't expect delays, I have a tendency to be a little more hesitant. I like things to happen in the right order, to be ready for them, to clear the decks before embarking on a new venture. This reflects the way my mother had prepared for my birth. Ean, on the other hand, will often simply do something apparently without thinking. He is much more likely to buy something on impulse, something he does not perhaps really need or even want, whilst I will think about a new purchase for some time before buying. From the outside it looks as though we act in the same way, but internally we listen to different drummers.

Before moving to Scotland in the summer of 1997 we spent just one week in Glasgow, house-hunting. It was a cold and wet February week, and the rain didn't stop once. But, curiously, things began to happen quickly for us once we had decided to move. A friend telephoned us to tell us that he had just moved to Scotland himself. The day of our arrival he introduced us to an estate agent who had just the type of property we were looking for in the area we liked. We viewed the property, the two lower floors of a large Victorian townhouse, and within three days we had bought it. We had no doubts whatsoever. When we arrived to move in a few months later we saw that the upper two floors were also for sale. It took us exactly three days to decide, but then we bought them too.

Would it have been so easy to make these decisions if one of us had had a long and difficult birth? I doubt it. Under the same circumstances someone who has had a long and difficult birth, and therefore *expects* things to be hard, would perhaps have wanted to see lots of other properties first, had detailed surveys done and perhaps haggled too long over the asking price.

Many people who come for Rebirthing have been stuck for some time in difficult, seemingly insoluble situations from which there appears to be no exit. Invariably they have had a long birth, frequently with added complications.

Radically different birth patterns can be a source of conflict in relationships. If you compare your own birth pattern with those of people you know well you will reach a greater understanding of why at times you irritate one another or why you do not get on at all. This is also one of the reasons why children of the same family can have such very different behavior patterns. One child, perhaps a night birth, likes to stay up late, whilst another likes to rise early. One child just *cannot* be ready on time for school, whilst another even has time to play ball in the garden before setting out.

A typical birth pattern, perhaps the most common, is that of a normal period of being stuck followed by a rapid emergence into the world. You can recognize this pattern in people who cannot get themselves motivated, but when they eventually do want something, they want it *now*. These people get impatient when they have to wait at bus-stops or in shopping queues and they don't start studying for exams until the last couple of weeks beforehand.

Not everyone, of course, who had a fairly 'normal' birth grows up with a tendency to procrastinate followed by demands for quick action. This is because as we grow up we are taught certain ways of behaving by our parents and teachers. If children can always get what they want and when they want it, they are not going to learn the meaning and benefits of patience. If they are never asked to make a choice and stick with it they will not learn to discriminate and take responsibility for their choices when they do make them. A great many of the negative effects of the birth experience can be changed by education. Later in life, meditation, yoga and life-changing alternative therapies such as cranial osteopathy, kinesiology, homeopathy and acupuncture can all make a major contribution, as can the right kind of psychotherapy.

Having trained in various disciplines, I have found that Rebirthing is by far the most effective and immediate method of dealing with the negative manifestations of birth trauma. Much, however, depends on the practitioner. As with any therapy, *who* the therapist is is far more important than what technique they use. Look at their qualifications and don't work with someone unless you also like them and feel you can trust them.

The best qualification the client can bring to a Rebirthing session is a willingness to be open to the changes that breathing therapy will inevitably bring. This means putting skepticism and cynicism aside. You would think that anyone seeking therapy was open to change, but people often don't expect that they themselves will have to change in order to receive the beneficial effects of therapy.

Again and again someone will interrupt the session and ask, 'Is this really working?' instead of allowing the experience to unfold and the breathing to do its transformative work. Doubt is an insidious saboteur, it creeps in when we are not looking, whispering in our ear that what we are doing is useless or that the person we are doing it with is no good. Often it is necessary to address this saboteur before any Rebirthing work can have an effect. On the other hand it can also happen that a cynical doubter has such a powerful experience of the numinous during a Rebirthing session that they are fundamentally changed by it.

The reason Rebirthing and other bodywork therapies can have such life-changing effects is because they activate a person's own healing powers rather than simply treat symptoms.

I have just observed two men working in my garden trying to unblock the main drain. They fed a wide hosepipe into the drain as far as it could reach. Then they turned on a powerful water jet, driven by a motor in their lorry, and within minutes the drain was clear. Previous attempts to unblock it had failed. What was needed was this extra pressure and power. This is how Rebirthing works, too. Through the breathing, you build up pressure inside. When enough energy has accumulated, it starts to move upward from your feet and flushes out every obstacle in its path. Your exhale then carries off the burned-up waste.

The fact that you can actually feel cleansed and lighter at the end of the session proves this theory. Your eyes look brighter, your limbs move with greater ease and you feel generally 'clean' inside. Even heavy smokers can breathe more freely and have far more space in their chests after a session.

Chris was visiting Britain and was persuaded by a friend to see me. She had no idea why she needed to come, as she was happy, healthy and free of problems. But she did not want to disappoint her friend and so went along with the suggestion. She was a bit embarrassed as she could not see the point of lying there and just breathing. But she continued, and she breathed well and deeply. At the end she sat up and said, 'So, what am I supposed to be feeling now?' I made her some herbal tea and we talked a little. Her smile widened and widened as we spoke. Then she said, 'You know, I am feeling extraordinarily well! Goodness, it is bright. The sun has come out!' It hadn't. I mentioned to her that people often see the world much more brightly after a session. It was only then that she admitted that her eyes had been giving her trouble. 'Everything used to look as if it was behind a grey veil.' This demonstrates again that the breath-energy will go the part that most needs healing, as if it had a consciousness of its own.

One little girl was brought to me because something had been troubling her which she was unable to talk about and her mother thought that perhaps Rebirthing could bring the problem into the open. The girl showed distress from time to time during the session, which lasted about thirty minutes, but basically it went smoothly. When she had finished she smiled and climbed onto her mother's lap, gave her a hug and said, 'I don't need to talk about it any more.' What had bothered her was simply not there any longer.

CELLULAR MEMORY

Many practitioners who work with releasing trauma and tension from the body, such as cranial osteopaths and polarity, past-life and regression therapists to name but a few, believe that memory is stored in cells and muscle tissue. The traditional medical view has been that only the brain can store memory, but this belief has recently been challenged. But how could a piece of body tissue possibly have a memory?

Deepak Chopra tells us in his excellent book *Quantum Healing* that our cells indeed have a kind of memory system, that they can pick up and send signals and that they are infinitely sensitive to receiving our thoughts. For instance it takes a hundredth of a second for a thought to reach a cell in your big toe. When you think about it you will see at once that each part of a healthy body knows exactly what it has to do. We do not have to think about *how* to pick up a pencil – the thought alone will activate the hand's memory of how to pick up an object. On the other hand, if you were told to pick up a pencil with your toes you might encounter a few problems. Your toes do not have the memory of how to pick up a pencil, but you could train them to do so and in time they too would remember. This is borne out by the incredible skills demonstrated by people without arms who paint by holding the brush in their feet or their mouths.

John E. Upledger, a cranial osteopath, in his book *Your Inner Physician and You* talks of *tissue memory*. He has found that when patients release tension in an area of the body where in the past they had sustained an injury, the memory of the incident would also return. At a lecture he once gave he was challenged by a psychologist who asserted that muscles couldn't possibly possess independent memory, that somehow the brain memory of the injury had been activated instead. Luckily there was also a physicist in the audience. Upledger writes:

> *The physicist simply reminded us of the fact that we could store a symphony on something as simple as a piece of plastic tape, and a total TV program complete with colour and sound on something just a little more complex but still of simple plastic. Therefore ... it seemed to make sense that something as complex as a muscle tissue, a bone or a piece of liver could store the memory of an accident or an injury.*

The most striking example, perhaps, of tissue memory is the famous case of a woman who received a heart transplant and afterwards developed a craving for fish and chips and beer. When she discovered who the donor had been she was not too surprised to find out that he loved just these things.

Removing the Birth Memory

I believe that the memory of our birth is also stored in our bodies rather than the brain, for whilst we do not consciously remember our birth, the memory frequently comes back to us during a Rebirthing session. For most people their birth was a struggle and often painful and frightening. The elimination of its memory from the body-mind system can greatly speed up a person's development. This was the original aim of Rebirthing.

We have already learned that our birth pattern affects us deeply, mostly in a negative way. It interferes with how we wish to live our lives consciously. Removing this birth memory from our bodies then would also remove the *source* of some of the difficulties we experience. This is precisely what happens. Rebirthing *speeds up lives*. It takes you from point A to B along the shortest possible route, the line of least activity. During a session, when a person continues to breathe *through* the return of the birth memory, *it is released completely*. So it ceases to have power and can no longer block the natural flow of life. It exists henceforth only as an ordinary memory, without an emotional charge.

BIRTH DREAMS

Although we may not consciously remember our birth, the unconscious memories may surface as dreams, many of them recurring and frightening. A common theme is finding oneself in a perilous situation, such as being stuck in a tunnel, in danger of falling from a great height, being in a fire or drowning. The dreamer always wakes before whatever they fear actually happens.

Up until the age of about twelve I had such a recurring dream. In this dream it is night-time and I am walking along a lonely path holding on to the fence on my left. I can see the light at the end of the path, but as I get nearer I know that what is at the end of the path is a long drop and at the bottom is a fiery furnace waiting for me. I know I shall fall into it and burn to death. Before I reached the end I would always wake up, screaming.

Another recurring nightmare I had was also concerned with birth (and perhaps also conception), but not my personal birth. This dream would start with absolute and petrifying nothingness – that is the only way I can describe it – and complete silence. Then they would come into the empty space, one by one ... the snakes. The white ones would enter the round hall from the left and the black ones from the right. Then they would fight for a long time until they were completely intertwined, forming one large snake. Again, this dream would wake me and I would seek my parents' bed for comfort, so great was my horror of these images. It was only a few years ago that I read in a book on mythology that this is how the great snake who gave birth to the world was created. So, as a child I had a repeated archetypal dream about birth, but there was no one at the time who could help me understand it.

Children especially have recurring nightmares related to birth. One should let them talk about them and even encourage them to relive them by talking about the events as if they were all happening in the present. This would take away a lot or even all of the fear. Drawing the nightmare and then getting a child to talk about the picture can also be a most effective way of bringing the nightmares to an end. The point is that you take a frightening inner image and place it outside yourself, where it can be looked at and talked about, and thus lose its power.

Rebirthing also provides an opportunity to re-enter and relive a birth dream and take it to its natural conclusion. The terrible things that we are afraid of never happen and the individual is helped to stay with the perilous situation until a natural shift occurs.

In my own case, during an active imagination exercise, I finally summoned up enough courage to let myself fall into the furnace. At the bottom was a spiral slide which I sped down and then found myself in beautiful countryside, happy and contented. I was in my thirties when I did this and I wish that I could have done this when much younger.

People who re-experience their birth during a Rebirthing session remark on how similar the actual experience is to the nightmare images. Peter felt that he was stuck in a tunnel, water was rushing past him, there was no light at the end and he thought he would never get out and would die. Virginia found herself sliding over an edge, holding on with her hands as hard as she could. She, too, thought she would fall and die. In a Rebirthing session, she was eventually able to let go and fall. But she did not die – she landed on soft grass instead.

Sometimes people only re-experience the physical symptoms associated with birth. Ina suddenly felt very hemmed in, as if she was being squeezed very tightly. Jackie felt herself thrashing against an obstacle. She was inside something and thought she would never get any further. She did not associate this with her birth until she saw the inside of the womb and then a fiery vagina. She had a very long birth and it sounds from her description as though she was in the wrong position for some time.

Dreams are the language of the unconscious and they try and tell us in picture or cartoon language what we need to know. Recurring dreams are an indication that we don't understand the message. Jung once said that everything in our lives can wait except our dreams. By taking our dreams seriously, by writing them down, by drawing them and, to gain even deeper insight, by imagining that each part of the dream is a part of ourselves, we will, in time, be able to decipher the dream's message for us.

DIFFERENT TYPES OF BIRTH

Quite apart from our dreams, the kind of birth we had affects our expectations of and attitudes towards life and the way we behave in crisis situations. Even if the birth goes relatively smoothly, certain aspects of it will leave their imprint on the young psyche and influence behavior.

Fast Birth

As already mentioned, those who had a fast birth like things to happen quickly. They tend to be early for everything – or at least on time. They can be impatient and strongly dislike waiting for anyone or anything. Waiting makes them anxious. 'Time and tide await no man' is their motto and they stick by it. They cannot understand why people do not plan enough in advance to be where they said they would be at the time arranged. Before setting out on a journey they like to plan the route carefully in order to avoid delays by taking wrong turns. Whenever possible they will take the easy way out, provided that the short-cut does not put them at a disadvantage. They can work very hard, but will still look for the quickest and most comfortable way of getting a job done. They definitely do not enjoy lingering without a purpose.

Ragnar, my youngest child, was a very fast birth. Contractions started at 5:30 in the morning and he was born at eight o'clock. When I arrived at the hospital I asked to have a hot bath and then lay down on my bed and breathed quietly. Nobody had any idea that I was about to give birth, so I was largely left alone. When the midwife did come to check the dilation of the cervix, Ragnar was already on his way. Within minutes she had to catch him as he shot out. Everything went perfectly well – the nurses were kind, I had a room to myself and I was looking forward to the rest. (My daughter Anna, only twenty-two months older than Ragnar, had broken a leg the previous week, which had meant sleepless nights and a great deal of extra work.)

But the very fast birth left its marks. As a child Ragnar had difficulty acquiring new skills. He expected to be able to ride a bicycle simply by sitting on it and to hit the ball with a tennis racquet perfectly the first time he tried. When he could not do so immediately he would blame it on the bicycle or the racquet. He simply did not have the patience to keep trying until he had mastered the new skill. Even during Rebirthing sessions, people who were born quickly display impatience. After only a few minutes of breathing they frequently say, 'There is nothing happening. When is it going to start?' These people have to be reassured that they can take all the time in the world, that there is nowhere to 'get to,' that it is *safe* for them to take their time.

The reason they are so anxious is that birth is a matter of life and death and how we are born becomes our survival tactic. So, if you are born quickly, speed is important to you when you are in difficulty or under pressure. If things do not progress quickly, the situation does not feel right and is soon abandoned.

Ragnar is now in his fourth year at university and it is also his fourth university. Each time he switched it was because he felt he wasn't getting anywhere with his studies or because he was convinced that he had chosen the wrong course. Not once did it occur to him that his lack of progress might have been due to his lack of patience and staying power. He is now realizing he needs to change, but only because he is beginning to run out of time. His birth pattern is that it all happens in the last couple of hours. Therefore, naturally, there is plenty of time. Birth has taught him that changes happen fast when they do happen.

It is true that when the conditions are right things do just happen for people who were born very quickly. After all, when life outside the womb began for them, it began suddenly, without much fuss or delay, and without any holding back. So, the pattern continues – if the timing is right for a fast birther, life just falls into place. Such people can be very lucky from time to time and it is quite fascinating to watch the way they get new situations together. One minute everything looks the same but the next moment all plans have changed and the first few steps to transforming their lives have already been taken, often without anyone else knowing about it.

The Long Labor

People who endured long labors, on the other hand, always seem to take longer over everything they do, no matter how hard they try. A slow birth indicates that the exit was blocked and that the baby had to struggle to get out. So life itself becomes a struggle. Such people often encounter delays and problems, they have a tendency to be late for appointments or are so anxious about *not* being late that they are far too early. They sometimes don't want to be on planet Earth at all.

Tim is in his fifties and came for a whole series of sessions. His mother was in labor with him for more than two days and he was finally delivered by forceps. He breathed well and needed little support. But he never once actually re-experienced his birth. At the end of a session he always felt unfinished. His whole life long he has felt unfinished. He can spend hours each day doing apparently nothing at all. He cannot keep order in his own home, as he has no energy to finish anything, not even the washing up. Occasionally he will make an attempt to tidy up his home, but will soon lapse back into 'not making it.' For Tim, survival is associated with *not* getting there, *not* coming out, *not* being born, because being born meant almost being killed.

Tim is an extreme case, as is Hans, whose mother was also in labor with him for several days and who was also a forceps delivery. Hans had hardly any energy to breathe at all. He needed constant encouragement to stay awake. His whole life had been lived in a low-key manner. He had not expected anything of himself or others. Yet there was also a tiny part of him that wanted to become free from this pattern. He kept coming for sessions, just like Tim, undeterred by the fact that he was 'not getting there.' Both Tim and Hans finally had a breakthrough which changed their lives, but it took them quite a few sessions longer than the average person and they can still lapse into total apathy from time to time.

Long labor individuals often feel that they cannot make it on their own, that they need help. The thought here is: 'I need to struggle in order to survive.' So the struggle becomes the most important thing and is often accompanied by a sense of hopelessness and the belief that without help one will not achieve anything.

Not all slow birthers show the above characteristics, however. Much depends on how the situation around and immediately after the birth was handled. Some people develop infinite patience. They *expect* things to take a long time to reach fruition. They are not in a hurry and they allow themselves to take as long as is needed. But in my experience these people are the exception.

The Breech Birth

When a baby's buttocks or feet are born first we call it a breech birth. Whether or not this is severely traumatic depends on many different factors. Even if all goes well and the birth takes an average length of time and no other difficulties are encountered a breech birth will leave its marks.

My first daughter, Stella, was a breech birth. She had been lying in the normal position, head down, until suddenly, on the day she was due to be born, she swung around and turned head upwards. The doctors lost no time bringing me into hospital and inducing labor, as they did not want her to get any bigger and thus complicate labor. I was looked after by a research team at one of the finest teaching hospitals in the UK, St Mary's Hospital, Paddington, and therefore had the best of care during my pregnancy. The labor itself was relatively easy. Throughout I did my special 'labor' breathing, as it was then taught by the Natural Childbirth Trust, and lay quietly, allowing my womb to do its work. I was surrounded by good-looking, young, mostly male medical students who attended to all my needs. They were quite impressed with the effect the rhythmic breathing was having.

Another woman was in labor in the bed next to mine. She was in great pain and cried and screamed a lot. She had forgotten to do her breathing exercises, she told me later. She went into the final stages of labor before I did and suddenly all the students disappeared to observe her giving birth in the delivery room. I was left alone and soon went into the final stage myself. It was quite an extraordinary experience. I felt as if my body were being ripped apart and a strange noise could be heard coming from my mouth, like that of a tortured animal.

I continued to support myself with breathing and, finally, after what seemed like ages, they all came back. The doctor examined me and the next thing I knew they were pushing my bed down the corridor at high speed towards the delivery room. I had started delivering my baby and there was no time to be lost. The advantage of being looked after by a research team is that you get the best doctors and as it happened mine was an expert in the *Kunstgriff*, a German word for a special twist with which a baby that is the wrong way round is turned out of the womb with nothing more than the use of hands.

The breathing had relaxed me sufficiently for my pelvic bones to soften and for the birth to proceed as speedily and in as trouble free a manner as possible. Within seconds of Stella's birth she lay in my arms, blood still on her face, eyes wide open and smiling, yes, smiling! We just lay there for a long time, gazing into each other's faces like two lovers finally reunited after years of separation. This was one of the most precious moments in my life and I think only another mother can really know what I mean. The medical team watched in silent appreciation. And Stella looked beautiful. (Breech babies have almost perfectly round heads as they have not been squeezed and crushed during birth to the same extent.) After a while her big blue eyes moved, following a nurse in a white coat around the room. Only then did they take her away to clean and dress her and return her to me again as soon as possible.

I have recounted this episode at some length to demonstrate that a breech birth need not be more traumatic for a baby than any other birth. What *was* traumatic for Stella, however, was having to have her hips X-rayed when she was only two days old, as inside the womb her legs had grown straight up the side of her body. Two attempts at X-raying were needed as she cried and struggled too much the first time. This episode was so upsetting for this two-day-old that she continued to have horrific nightmares about it right into adulthood. She kept dreaming that she was walking in a beautiful meadow full of daisies when suddenly a huge metal object came slowly down from the sky on top of her. She could not push it off and she knew it would crush her. She always awoke in great panic. Shortly after I had trained as a Rebirther I gave her a session and it was no surprise to me that this very scenario from the dream came up. We worked with it and the memory of being X-rayed re-emerged. Since then the nightmare has not reoccurred.

I have observed in Stella, and other breech births, that wrong turns can be taken at important junctures and wrong decisions can be made. This is because the baby will know that it is the wrong way round and will be aware that it is 'going the wrong way.' So, coming into the world means going in the wrong direction. These people often do not find the right way in life until after the age of thirty-five or forty, or sometimes even later. There is often a feeling that they are in the wrong job or on a path to nowhere. Whilst other people race past them on their way to the top the breech birth will get side-tracked into all kinds of other activities, either to delay, consciously or unconsciously, 'getting there,' or simply because they *cannot get it right.*

When Stella was a small child she would often do the opposite of what I asked her to do. She was not rebellious or deliberately disobedient, but if, for instance, I wanted her to sit in her pushchair and she kept getting out to run about, I would only have to ask her to stay out of the pushchair in order to get her to climb into it. I am sure that this was not an attempt on her part to defy me, as she would do this quite calmly, as if it were the most natural thing in the world. She was quite contrary. If I referred to the lovely yellow colour of the moon she would insist that the moon was pink but if I said the moon was blue she would say that it was yellow!

People displaying typical breech birth patterns feel that they have done everything 'back to front' in their lives. Even when they have found a career that suits them they often get diverted and try out other things simultaneously, just in case there is a better way. There seems to be a difficulty to commit to a specific direction.

During Rebirthing sessions these people find themselves sliding down, feet first, when birth approaches. This even happens to people who did not know that they were a breech birth.

The Planned Caesarean Birth

Planned Caesarean births are becoming more common, for the convenience of both mothers and doctors. Such a birth is also frequently necessary because of difficulties encountered during previous labors or because of some other complication that would otherwise put both mother and baby at risk. The medical profession considers Caesarean sections less risky than a vaginal delivery for some specific situations, e.g. a large baby presenting by the breech. Euan Laird quoted some figures from St Mary's, Paddington (the same hospital where my own breech birth daughter was so skillfully delivered without the aid of instruments), in which the mortality rate for breech births was twenty times greater for vaginal breech delivery than for a vaginal cephalic delivery.

The baby born by Caesarean section does not have to struggle and this does indeed appear to be the easiest way to be born. But let's look a little more closely. In a planned Caesarean no creative birth process takes place. There is too rapid a transition from inside the womb to the world outside. One minute the baby is happy and secure inside a warm womb and the next it is lifted out into an alien world. Sometimes the mother has even had a general anaesthetic and seems to be lifeless and there may be a lot of blood around.

So, a Caesarean birth can result in timidity and lack of confidence – 'I mustn't do it on my own' is the child's underlying reality. It can also cause separation anxiety – you never know what is going to happen next. After all, the baby's first experience of life was that of sudden separation from the habitat in which it had lived for a considerable length of time. However, so much, as always, depends on what happens immediately after birth. If the mother is not unconscious she can be there for her child, welcoming and comforting it, and thus mitigating, as with most other types of birth, the traumatic after-effects.

With a planned Caesarean there is no natural signal from the baby that this is its moment to enter the world. The birth day and time are largely determined by the hospital's, and sometimes the mother's, timetable. A curious phenomenon has been occurring for many years. With the increase of planned Caesarean births more and more children are born during daylight hours. I find this worrying, as for many souls their natural time of birth may be during the hours of darkness. These people often feel 'unborn' at the end of a Rebirthing session and frequently need to go through the process of birth several times before they can connect with the actual coming into the world.

Unplanned Caesarean Birth

Unplanned Caesarean births have different consequences from planned ones. Labor would have started in the normal way and at a time chosen by the baby, unless it was induced. But then something would have gone wrong, placing mother and/or baby in danger and requiring a Caesarean to be performed. Now this is quite a different story from a planned Caesarean birth, where no labor is involved at all. Here, both baby and mother, no matter how much they struggled, failed to bring about the birth. But they did try. Hormonal release would have been experienced by both mother and baby. It is the rush of adrenaline that gives a baby that great thrust to move forward and out. Just look at a newborn baby after it has worked its way out of the womb and you will see a small quivering pink body of tremendous energy.

The unplanned Caesarean birth can have very positive consequences because the baby's experience of the creative process is
that when the going gets really tough it will be rescued. Someone
will be there to safeguard both mother and child. Although people
born by unplanned Caesarean still have to struggle to get where
they want to, deep down inside they know that there will be help
at hand in the end. They can be extremely lucky in life. But much,
as always, depends on the circumstances surrounding the birth.
The best insurance policy for a happy start in life is immediate
close contact with the mother.

Cord around the Neck

Sometimes in the womb the umbilical cord becomes twisted
around the baby's neck, obstructing the life force in the throat area.
This is the creative centre according to the Eastern chakra system
and when we are blocked in the throat we cannot express ourselves
adequately. Babies born with the cord round their necks have often
had their throats restricted for quite a long time. When at birth the
cord is cut hastily, before the baby's lungs have started functioning
and it is breathing independently, it receives a double shock, as it
can experience the release of the cord as a life-threatening trauma.

A doctor at a recent health conference in Zürich told me that at
her hospital in cases where the cord appears to have been around
the neck for some time prior to birth, the doctors no longer cut it
immediately, but rather release it gradually, as that poses less risk
and trauma.

People born with the cord around their necks frequently feel
held back. They often feel cut off from their emotions, are unable
to assert themselves in relationships and report a sense of feeling
trapped in unhappy situations from which they see no way out.
Their fear is concentrated in the throat. The life force is choked.

People who have experienced this type of complication can be
afraid to expose their necks and like to wear clothes with high
necks and scarves for protection and comfort. The neck tends to

remain a sensitive area for them and when they get ill they feel it first in the throat. They need to learn to express themselves freely and allow themselves to take a few risks. I have found that Rebirthing therapy can open and free the throat area significantly, making spontaneous self-expression and a more liberated style of living possible.

Forceps Delivery

One of the most traumatic deliveries for both mother and baby is with forceps. To have one's head crushed by huge metal instruments and then pulled, maybe even twisted and turned, is a painful process. The baby emerges bruised and shocked and will need a great deal of comforting straightaway so that being forced into the world can be associated with a sense of belonging once the trauma is over.

Forceps people can be procrastinators. They were trapped during birth and the life and death situation demanded the actions of another person to ensure their survival. At the same time, though, that very help brought them even more pain and trauma. So, people born this way will wait and wait for something to happen that will compel them into action and will then resist any help. They may struggle and get stuck in life and need to be rescued, but they will neither ask for help nor want it when it arrives. They experience rescue as painful and would rather remain stuck than endure further pain. They feel that others cannot be trusted.

For forceps births a solution would be to create a compelling situation, if possible with a deadline. Ideally, they create their own pressure and find ways to strengthen their will to enable them to keep going when the going gets tough. Rebirthing will remove the birth trauma completely and therefore change these people's life patterns dramatically, *if* they will accept the help willingly.

I recently worked with a young woman who had a very long labor and which ended with a forceps delivery. She was extremely difficult to work with because she kept trying to sabotage her session by wanting to get up in the middle of it to have a cigarette. On the one hand she was eager to have her sessions and be released from an almost unbearable feeling that life was a permanent torture, but on the other she would cancel each appointment and reschedule. She had tried all manner of other therapies before but nothing seemed to have worked. The main problem was to keep her coming for sessions for long enough to achieve a real improvement.

Unfortunately she did not complete the course. But after her second session she began to talk about the very good future that she could have with her boyfriend if only she could lose her fear of life. This was a particularly poignant example of someone born by forceps delivery whose trust in 'helpers' (including me) seemed to have been so severely damaged that she could not possibly allow herself to stay in any therapy for long enough for a new birth to take place. For her, that would mean once again facing a life-threatening trauma, which this time she might not survive.

Attempted Abortion

It came as a great surprise to me when very early on in my work as a Rebirther, a young man called Jan, a psychotherapist himself, kept pulling up his legs in his first session and hiding his face behind his hands, then retreated against the wall and shouted: 'No, no, don't kill me, don't kill me!' He was clearly going through a most horrific attack of some kind and his yells became louder and more frantic. I went along with this for some time, then finally asked him what was going on. Almost too scared to speak and continuing to make himself smaller and smaller, he whispered, 'They are trying to kill me. My mother is trying to abort me.'

Since then I have Rebirthed other individuals who have suffered a failed abortion and this has completely changed my ideas on this whole issue. Medical science does not believe that a tiny foetus a few weeks old can feel pain, but these examples seem to suggest otherwise. There seems to be a consciousness that exists from the very beginning, that is continuous and is not dependent on the functioning of the physical brain.

Not surprisingly, people who survive abortion attempts feel rejected. They feel unwanted, unloved, unworthy and that they should not be here in the first place. There is a tendency to self-abuse and self-loathing. Such people seem to get into relationships where they assume the role of victim and no matter how much they *know* what they are doing to themselves, they cannot stop it. Survival depends on being rejected, as this was the original experience in *this* body. These people also have the belief that someone is out to 'get them,' to hurt them, even kill them. Trust is a major problem. They tend to attract people they cannot trust and therefore reinforce the original idea that they are not wanted and not worthy of support, love and respect.

Jan also contacted several past lives in which he had been abused, rejected and isolated from society. None of these was in any way glamorous. In one he experienced himself as a lone wolf, separated from his pack, but yearning for companionship. This particular session connected him with the depth of his isolation from others in this life and the huge despair that he could feel at times. In most past lives he made attempts to belong to an individual or a group and yet usually failed. After Rebirthing these negative memories out of his body-mind system, his life changed dramatically for the better. He eventually returned to Australia, his native land, where he is now successfully practicing psychotherapy.

In order for life to proceed joyfully and freely, the birth trauma – which includes life-threatening intrauterine experiences and all perinatal difficulties – needs to be removed completely from the cellular system of the body. Otherwise 'energy cysts,' or negative memories, will always present an obstacle to the flow of vital life force.

Unwanted Births

The effects of being born an unwanted child are not dissimilar to those of attempted abortions.

An example is Annie, who was twenty-eight when she realized she was carrying another child, her third. She was already three months pregnant and was horrified. She had never wanted more than two children, having grown up in a large family in southern Italy during the years following the Second World War, when money and food were scarce. She wanted her two children to have a better life and felt that it was irresponsible to bring more children into a world that showed increasing signs of not being able to support its growing population. In Annie's world view two children per family were ideal.

Shortly after she found out that she was pregnant again she tried to have an abortion but was unable to raise the finances. She also became extremely ill with a virus infection and for two months forgot all about being pregnant. Very slowly she regained her health and by the time she was six months pregnant had totally recovered. She had also moved to a much better and larger house and her husband had found new employment.

From about this time onwards she started to connect with her growing baby. She had always been a good mother and she was now looking forward to the birth, taking good care of herself for the baby's sake, and generally felt as radiant and well as she had when pregnant with her other two children. Her son, Max, was born without complications and was no trouble at all as a small baby. In fact he was so 'good' that he slept for seven hours on a trot, day and night. He did, however, need a whole hour when being fed.

Later, though, he grew into a problem child. Although he was receiving the same upbringing and education as Annie's other two children, he was extremely disruptive at home and at school and refused to co-operate with any group of people. He would separate himself even when quite small and in order to avoid playing games would sit on his own in a corner and look at picture books. He continued to be uncooperative until he was thirteen and went to boarding-school. His father had told him about his mother trying to abort him (though he most likely had always known at some subliminal level) and by then he was able to talk about how he felt: 'The problem is that I was never wanted, that I have never been loved and that I should not be here.'

When he came for Rebirthing, shortly before being accepted for university, the main issue for the first three sessions was a feeling of desperate loneliness and isolation, which he was able to release successfully. His mother told me recently that he still cuts a rather solitary figure but that he has finally found his goal in life. He wants to work in an animal sanctuary, preparing wild, injured and abandoned animals to be released back into their natural habitat. Thus, because of his own early experiences Max can identify with wounded and traumatized animals. But instead of merely feeling compassion he actually wants to get out there and help them live as normal a life as possible. It is not uncommon for people during Rebirthing to identify with other forms of life. During Max's first session he experienced being a dolphin. What this actually *means* I cannot say, but for the person having the Rebirth these are significant moments.

It seems that circumstances surrounding the very beginning of fetal life can have the most powerful effects and offer evidence that there is a mind, a consciousness, present that knows what is going on right from conception and records and stores all events.

When the mother rejects the baby throughout pregnancy and either continues to reject it after birth or has it adopted the situation can sometimes have such a negative effect on the growing child that it precipitates disturbing anti-social behavior and/or depressive and even psychotic tendencies.

I have only ever Rebirthed one case where being given away at birth had a happy outcome. I expected the client, Alice, to relive the rejection she had suffered when she was born. But instead a different picture emerged. From the moment of conception Alice knew that she did not want to be this woman's child, that she detested this womb and that she needed to do everything in her power to get away from her mother. 'If she gets hold of me she will abuse me and torture me as she has done before in another life,' she explained. When her mother did give her away to a home soon after birth Alice felt nothing but relief. Three months later she was adopted into a kind loving family who were also wealthy and able to provide her with a superb education.

The Wrong Sex

How many of us were expected to be of the opposite sex! This is a more common phenomenon than one would at first believe. In my own case my parents already had three girls when I came along. My mother was sure that I would be the longed-for boy. She even had a name for me, Frank, and a complete layette in blue. And how disappointed she was! I tried hard to be liked by not being a nuisance. As a baby I would sleep from feed to feed and rarely cried. As I grew up I liked to wear my hair extremely short and rode around on my bicycle in blue jeans and outsized sweaters. I was distinctly aware of disliking anything 'feminine' and devised a new fashion to suit the image I wanted to project, making myself garments that looked neither male nor female. My grandfather's three-quarter-length black woolen coat with a velvet collar became my winter overcoat, I used his old leather travelling case as my briefcase for school and wore my father's old sailing sweaters.

Of course I was unaware at the time why I was doing this. It felt like fun, made me look different and I soon developed a fashion which many other girls at school copied. I loved being with the boys and on school trips to the mountains and forests I would bribe them with sweets to let me be one of their gang. Whenever I was allowed to join them I felt extraordinarily happy. At school I excelled in chemistry, physics and mathematics – good solid male subjects. I shunned dancing, sewing and cooking, and couldn't possibly imagine why any woman would want to get married and have children.

As I grew older and had my first boyfriend this changed. If he said he loved the colour pink on a woman I would rush out and buy pink. He liked women with long hair, so I grew mine. He would write me little love-notes and I wrote some back. Gradually, but only very gradually, I learned that it could be alright, even fun, to be a woman. That I was valued for being female came as a complete surprise to me.

I wonder whether, if my mother had wanted a girl when she was pregnant with me, or at least had been neutral about it, I would have behaved more like a female from the start. Would I have dared to flirt with my father? Would I have acknowledged to myself that I was beautiful and that I noticed men looking at me? As it was I had to learn consciously how to be a woman. Men were my teachers. They let me know what they liked and I obliged, until I felt confident enough to create my own image according to how I felt inside.

In my work as a psychotherapist and Rebirther I have met many people, men and women, who were expected to be the opposite sex. This is more obviously noticeable in women. There is a general tendency with them to keep their hair short, to wear trousers, to be very thin and flat-chested and to feel *proud* to be in male company. For men this is perhaps a more difficult issue, for they cannot easily wear skirts or have long hair, although some of course do defy normal social mores and do precisely that. Most men who feel 'all wrong' tend to hide their feelings, but they manifest as lack of achievement, suppression of potential, fear of striving and risking and, above all, a lack of self-assertion. In order to be loved, these men feel that they cannot be who they are, they are just 'not good enough.'

The 'wrong' sex may even turn out to be the right sex. One woman went to see a fortune-teller and was told that she would soon be pregnant and that it would be a boy. She totally accepted this prediction and prepared herself to welcome a male child by talking to the 'little man' inside her, buying blue clothes and generally getting used to the fact that the child she was carrying was male. When she gave birth to a girl instead she was overjoyed, but she had not allowed herself to voice her preference whilst pregnant, lest it upset the 'boy.' I believe that the baby would have known that she was the right sex for the mother and that she would be a lovely surprise. It always surprises me when during a Rebirth someone remembers, or reports at least, what the parents' desires and expectations were. The father's expectations as to the sex of the baby seem to make more of an impression after it is born. At least I have never come across a case where someone felt before birth that they were the wrong sex for the father.

I have painted here a general picture; as always, so much depends upon what happens once the baby enters this world and there are many other circumstances that can affect the newborn's future life.

Illegitimacy

Until the 1960s, when the sexual revolution began, illegitimacy was frowned upon. People born out of wedlock knew that there was something not quite right with them and would try to keep the truth of their birth from others. These people often did not get married or married late and tended to have illegitimate children themselves.

A good example of this pattern was Joan, an unmarried mother, who was born out of wedlock. When her mother became pregnant, she was disowned by her parents and tried to keep her pregnancy a secret by covering up with loose clothing. Joan grew up with a fear of being discovered. She chose to work unofficially, not registering with any authority, because she felt – partly unconsciously – that if 'they' found out that she existed she would be in deep trouble. She made a good living, working undercover, and also brought up a child successfully. Secretly, though, she yearned to be 'legitimate,' which was her reason for seeking therapy. Her catastrophic expectations turned out to be vastly exaggerated, for when she finally sought legal advice and became a 'legitimate' member of society, there were no problems at all. She eventually married, studied law and is now 'legitimately,' and very successfully, working in the legal profession.

Fortunately, since Joan was born things have changed and illegitimacy is no longer a problem. Single parenthood is a phenomenon of modern society, not a stigma.

The Mother Holds Back

Sometimes it happens that the baby tries to be born at a time that is not convenient. When my sister started labor with her second child her husband rushed her to hospital in their Volkswagen. There were many red traffic lights on the way and the baby was in a hurry. My sister squeezed her thighs together as hard as she could, appealing to the baby not to come just yet. But finally it was all to no avail and her daughter was born there and then on the front seat of the car.

This is not a particularly severe or dramatic case of being held back. Others are far more serious, as when the mother screams during labor every time the baby moves. This situation is quite common. When the birth memory is activated, such people can remember being afraid to push and struggle in case it would hurt their mother. Later in life, also, they will not ask for what they want or assert themselves or live their own lives in case it hurts someone else (particularly the mother). These people feel held back, unable to push themselves into the foreground or receive the attention they so desperately need and want. To be powerful, to use their power, would be experienced as harmful.

Much also depends on the care the baby receives after birth. Most people still think that babies don't understand anything, that time will heal all wounds, that the birth trauma will pass. This attitude is born out of great ignorance. If we knew that the baby recorded every second of its life during its stay in the womb and during and after birth, we would perhaps treat the newborn infant with greater understanding and respect, and administer more appropriate after-care, as we do to any adult who has suffered a life-threatening shock. We think that as long as baby sleeps it is alright, but sleep is often an escape from further trauma.

Incubator Babies

My experience with people who spent some time immediately after birth in an incubator is that they have to be born twice. That is to say, they need to experience their emergence from the womb and then again later from the incubator. They frequently feel cut off from the world. There is a lack of sensation of bodily feeling, as physical touching was initially kept to a minimum, and a sense that they are surrounded by an invisible wall.

Also, as they were placed in an incubator for their survival, these people believe that they need to be separated from others in order to survive. This may manifest as shyness, uncertainty and lack of confidence in how to be one's own person. Such people can appear aloof and fearful of relating to others in an intimate way. In relationships they are often extremely dependent on the partner.

Twins

There are just as many different births for twins as there are for single births, but there is always the added factor of the companion in the womb and during birth. Just as a single baby lives a life of mystical participation with the mother, so twins share a life that is as one. During birth, though, complications can occur.

What happened to Gemma is not uncommon. Her brother was born first but because of the size of his head he got stuck in the birth canal. During Rebirthing Gemma clearly remembered panicking and pushing like mad and thinking that she was going to die. She suffered from claustrophobia for much of her life. Men appeared to her selfish and always wanting to put themselves first, but at the same time she adored them and clearly thought them superior to women. She felt she had to appease men, keep them well disposed towards her, as she might come to harm if she didn't.

If she could keep them moving in a friendly way she would not get stuck behind them again.

Kim, another client, also had a twin brother. But he was much smaller than her. 'He never really grew,' she told me sadly during one Rebirth. He died inside the womb shortly before birth. Kim emerged first and never saw her brother again. We had to do a great deal of grief work as she had totally suppressed the pain of losing her companion along the way to birth. Kim eventually realized that her brother had only come along this far to make sure she would not be alone during her time in the womb. When she could finally accept how much her brother had meant to her, how close they had been and how much she still loved him, she was able to cry for the first time during our work together. This emotional catharsis had the most profound healing effect on her. It was especially important as Kim had also spent a couple of weeks in an incubator after birth and had always felt cut off from her feelings.

Another client of mine relived the trauma of being inside the womb with a twin brother who had died. This dead baby became her companion. She became attached to him and was traumatized when he disappeared at birth. As a result of this bizarre attachment and subsequent loss, she developed an overdependent behavior pattern. Her need for closeness and attention was experienced as too demanding and too unrealistic by her string of boyfriends, who felt totally unable to deal with her demands. We worked for three sessions on this issue before she could feel able to let go of this need for constant reassurance and consuming separation anxiety.

The above examples all demonstrate how time spent in the womb and the conditions surrounding birth can leave deep imprints on our soft and wide-open psyches. My work with birth memory has completely reoriented my views on pregnancy, birth and the immediate after-care of the newborn. With so much empirical evidence now available from Rebirthers, past-life therapists and holotropic breathworkers from around the world, we can no longer deny that even the foetus is in possession of a mind and a memory system that records the minutest details of everything that is happening to it and that predates brain memory.

Breathworkers the world over also know that when negative birth memories are removed by the cleansing properties of the breath they no longer cause trouble and interfere with the natural flow of the universal life force within us. When a piece of memory has been removed there is space for a creative realignment of psychic components to take place. It is this psychic shift that brings about the necessary changes in our outer lives.

PART 2

REBIRTHING AND PAST-LIFE THERAPY

7 THE QUESTION OF REINCARNATION

Sri Krishna:
You and I, Arjuna,
Have lived many lives.
I remember them all:
You do not remember.
Bhagavad Gita

We were not taught about past lives in our Rebirther training, so it had not occurred to me that this would become a major part of my work. During the training we concentrated on directing the relaxed exhale through the various bodily sensations that could manifest during sessions, not on finding out what these might be about. But I had a solid grounding in various therapies that used the imagination, therapies that pay particular attention to the memories, tensions, emotions and stories that are held in the body, so when someone started feeling tension in their body I would ask them to explore it more deeply, feel it more strongly and even exaggerate it and let an image, colour or shape emerge.

What people held in these tight places, these 'energy cysts,' were first of all childhood events that had not seemed particularly important at the time, but, when explored more fully, often held profound unexpressed grief. Then, as we worked more deeply, directing the breath more powerfully or deeply to a particular area in the body, birth traumas surfaced, followed by the intrauterine life before birth. But then it all changed for me. Spontaneously, without warning, important events from past lives also began to emerge. I felt I had stumbled upon something extremely important, something that seemed to demand release into consciousness.

It was during a hot-tub weekend that I first came across past-life retrieval. Hot-tub Rebirthing takes place, as the name suggests, in a hot tub – a pool of hot bubbling water, large enough to hold three people, plus one or two attendants each. It is generally expected that you enter the pool naked to facilitate the emergence of very early experiences. You use a snorkel to breathe and lie face down in the water. The attendant supports you lightly under your belly and you start your conscious connected breathing. After about twenty minutes you begin to feel the energy moving, the rush of pranic force, libido, what is also often referred to as kundalini energy.

Once the energy movement is under way the Rebirthee gets out of the tub and into a hot shower, where the breathing continues. After the shower they are wrapped in warm toweling robes and encouraged to lie down and rest. Now the material that is fast emerging as a result of the water-rebirth, material that may be connected with life inside the uterus and immediately after birth, will be processed, that is, discussed with the facilitator.

On my first occasion in the hot tub I was teamed with a woman in her mid-twenties. I was to attend her in the pool first. She was an experienced breather, having done many more training seminars than I had, and she soon felt the energy surge. We left the hot tub and went together into the hot shower, but almost immediately she wanted the water to be cooler and cooler until it was freezing cold (I was in the shower breathing with her the whole time). At first she seemed to enjoy the icy water but then she got agitated, started whimpering and finally screamed and screamed as if she had gone mad. I knew that I was in the presence of something odd, something altogether different from ordinary Rebirths. Whilst it did not frighten me – in fact, I was fascinated – the experience was nevertheless spine-chilling. The noises that the woman was so powerfully producing did not sound like those of a human being, more like those of a tortured animal.

The screaming and howling beneath the cold flow of water continued for a few minutes. Then the woman demanded: 'I need to hang. I need to hang on something!' We got out of the shower and she found the railings that led around the top of the hot-tub room. She climbed up and suspended herself from these and continued her screaming for a few more minutes, with me watching patiently and with great interest.

When she had calmed down I wrapped her up warmly, laid her down on a foam mattress and put my arms around her. Eventually she was able to speak. She told me she had gone back to a past life in which she had been accused of being a witch. One of the ways in which they judged whether you were a witch or not was by tying you to a ducking-chair, lowering you from a bridge into the cold water of the river beneath and keeping you under. When the chair was raised again, and you had drowned, you were innocent, but if you were still alive it was a sign that you had supernatural powers and were therefore in league with the Devil, so you were found guilty. They would then either burn you at the stake (as they did in France), hang you or, as happened in this case, string you up and kill you by disemboweling you or driving a stake through your belly. Having survived the ducking-chair and been found guilty of witchcraft this woman had been suspended from a tree with her arms and legs tied apart. Then they cut open her torso and emptied it out.

Past lives can haunt us and influence our behavior and our relationships in many and harmful ways. In this case the memory of an event which took place more than two hundred years ago was still being carried within this woman's body-memory, with all its attendant horror, emotion and bodily sensation. Little did I know how important this experience was to become not only in shaping my future work as a Rebirther but also in finding out about my own previous incarnations.

During my training nothing like this happened again. I had to wait until I began my independent work as a Rebirther to discover the hidden stories behind people's sophisticated twentieth-century lives. Once I started working seriously and regularly as a Rebirther, though, the emergence of past lives became a regular event. Synchronistically, my husband brought home a copy of a fascinating book: *Other Lives, Other Selves* by Roger Woolger, who was a fellow student of his when they were both training to become Jungian analysts at the Jung Institute in Zürich. When I read Roger's book I found that he was making observations identical to my own. Furthermore, to my amusement, a client of mine would have a particular past-life experience one day and the next I would read about it in the book. The opposite also happened: I would read Roger's description of a particular past-life phenomenon and the very next day, or hour even, someone would go through precisely that experience. I knew without a doubt that I was on the right track. Jungian synchronicity, or meaningful coincidence, was certainly at work here. Synchronistic events have a tendency to start happening in increasing numbers when one is on the correct trail.

I recognized without any difficulty that the past lives being uncovered were not just the products of people's morbid or fanciful imagination, but were very real and extremely important. I seemed to have no choice but to find someone who could teach me more about reincarnation. Without hesitation, I enrolled in Roger Woolger's training and completed it within one year.

The training was invaluable for two reasons. First, Roger is a superb teacher and I learned a tremendous amount from him and all the participants of the past-life workshops. Secondly, because I was already an experienced Rebirther by the time I entered the training, I was able to apply conscious connected breathing during past-life therapy sessions, whether I was receiving the therapy myself or facilitating someone else. As a result I found that the breathing provided additional power, enabling people to complete each past-life therapy session satisfactorily, feeling calm, relaxed and cleansed of the old memories. This is not always the case if breathing is not part of the therapy, as I have witnessed many times. In other words, if the person on the receiving end of a past-life Rebirthing session included circular rhythmic breathing as a way of accessing and cleansing old memory patterns, they would feel that an important piece of work had been completed, magically removed from their body-mind systems, without the need to continue further work on this particular issue. Subsequently, whenever appropriate, I combined the two methods with highly satisfactory results, whether in individual sessions or in group situations.

THE PURPOSE OF REMEMBERING

People often ask me whether it is not perhaps a little too traumatic to relive our past lives. Shouldn't we leave those memories buried where they are and not upset ourselves? How can remembering something like this possibly be good for us? What good does it do anyway? Shouldn't we be concentrating on *this* life rather than on the past?

These are valid and interesting questions, and I used to ask them too. Before I knew about tissue or cellular memory none of what I learned from Rebirthing would have made any sense. But as, one after the other, people regained memories of lives in other times and other cultures, it gradually dawned on me that this was nothing unusual really, that every person has lived many lives. These are part and parcel of our general memory system, but they are deeply buried within the body-mind and therefore not part of our consciousness. So, reliving a past-life scenario that was traumatic and unfinished does not *cause* a further trauma but *releases* it. Unreleased, it would remain festering in the unconscious, perhaps doing untold damage or interfering with our conscious purpose.

This is why often we don't even know what it is that prevents us from living our lives in the manner that we should. Our frustrations, delays, unhappiness, illnesses and lack of success may seem inexplicable. But if we breathe on a problem, if we breathe on an energy block, we can dispel it. In the words of the thirteenth-century mystic poet Jalal al-Din Rumi, 'You breathe upon a piece of clay, [and] it becomes either a dove or a kite.'

It is not simply a matter of raising the past-life trauma to consciousness, but also one of ensuring a psycho-spiritual release from your whole body-mind or cellular system. This is why the combination of Rebirthing and past-life therapy is so potent. It is the breath that takes us deep into past-life memories, it is the breath that releases them and brings them to consciousness and it is the breath that cleanses each and every particle out of the body-mind's complex system. When an episode is successfully 'completed' you will *know* that something has gone, and gone for good. It will remain only as a memory, without emotional charge and without any power to control the direction of your life.

So, remembering a past life and 'breathing' it out, does no harm at all; on the contrary, it does a lot of good. It actually speeds up and facilitates the flow and direction of the present life. As long as negative effects from a past life are buried deep within the unconscious, they can hinder a person's development, stifle creativity and be disempowering. They can make someone timid, bitter, cruel and even stupid, depending on the type of experience. Unfinished business is also quite frequently the cause of irrational fears and phobias. The following example from my own life, although not the most dramatic, serves as a clear example.

Ever since I can remember I have been afraid of exposing my neck. From childhood I would prefer to wear high-necked sweaters and blouses; I would sleep with my hands covering my neck. I also had a recurring nightmare in which I was alone in a prison cell and I knew that the following morning they would take me in a cart to the guillotine and that I would have my head chopped off. This dream appeared to me with great regularity and it always took me a while to shake it off after waking. I was in dread of this nightmare recurring until one day, in a Rebirthing session, I relived a scenario from a past life during the French Revolution. In that life I had been a young woman; the murderous revolutionary regime was a threat to my family and we went into hiding. But someone betrayed us and as a result we all lost our heads. Since reliving this event the nightmare has not recurred nor am I any longer afraid of exposing my neck.

Another nightmare, which began to make a regular appearance when my children were young, was one in which I went to the doctor with an eye problem and he cut my head off as a cure. I was devastated as I could now no longer see my children. I would always wake from this dream deeply depressed, but no matter how much I tried to analyze the dream no meaning suggested itself. Since the recovery of that French life this nightmare has stopped, too; it seems to have been a modern variation on losing my head in the eighteenth century.

In a later past-life Rebirthing session I actually relived the execution – in slow motion and therefore great detail. My hands were tied behind my back. I felt very calm and prepared to meet my death. As I bent over, I heard the guillotine come crashing down and felt my head come off. Then I floated above my body and saw the severed head lying on the ground. It was strange to see myself there without a head. I had no attachment to this body that I had just left. But, fortunately, the therapist encouraged me to gather up the head and put it back in its place. This I did; it took a few minutes before I could feel sure that the head was secure and that the image would not change back to the previous one. All the while I was using the breath to complete each stage. Finally, my body restored to wholeness, I could finish with that life and leave it behind without regrets.

Interestingly, I often spontaneously speak and think in French, usually in private, to my children or my husband. When I do so I feel both psychologically and physically a different person. Although I learned French in school and spent up to a year at a time in a French-speaking country, as well as travelling extensively through France, I do not think that this is the reason for my lapses into French, for I also learned Spanish and travelled through Spain, but only speak it when I need to.

THE NEAR-DEATH EXPERIENCE

When people relive a death from a past life the experience is identical in many details to what is known as the 'near-death experience.' Near-death experiences have been reported by people all over the world and from all religious backgrounds and much research has been conducted into them. They occur most often when a person's life is in danger, as in an accident or whilst undergoing an operation.

Most near-death experiences have several factors in common, for example floating above the body, travelling down a tunnel at high speed, finding a very bright light at the end of the tunnel, meeting a benign, loving figure and receiving some kind of knowledge and insight that considerably changes the attitude to life. Again, these experiences are now so numerous, and can no longer be explained away as chemical changes in the brain, that we need to begin to accept them as a fact of life.

BELIEF AND EVIDENCE

Some people, of course, do not believe that we live life after life and will try to explain away any experience to the contrary. Personally, I don't doubt for one moment that we have lived through many lives before and that many lives still lie before us. But it is not the purpose of this book to try and prove reincarnation. There are many good books available that deal with research into past lives. A few years ago, Ean made a six-part series for BBC2 entitled *Is There Something After Death?*, one of the very first programs to treat this question seriously. We were sent books about past lives and about how to die a good death from people all over the world and for many weeks I had the opportunity to read extensively about this subject. At the time I had no idea that one day I would work with people on their past lives and the deaths that they had encountered therein.

Perhaps the best evidence so far that we have lived before comes from very young children who speak about their 'real' families and 'other' homes and who have 'imaginary' friends who are as real to them as other members of the family. If these children are not talking about previous existences, what are they talking about? They are too young to know anything about other countries and other cultures, yet some of their past-life accounts show unmistakably that they are familiar with the mores and the language of the country they consider their 'real' home. Dr Peter Fenwick of London University, who together with his wife Elizabeth is conducting his own extensive research, says that past-life recall in children peaks between the ages of four and seven and then fades away. The skeptic would say that these children are tuning into a collective memory reservoir that seems to be floating like a huge cloud through the universe. I find this notion even more bizarre than the idea of reincarnation.

Some people believe that they have lived before but have only had one or two lives and that this one is definitely their last – meaning that they do not need to come back to acquire more knowledge and wisdom. I tell such people that they still have many, many lives before them and quote the Buddha: 'Until the last blade of grass is enlightened I shall return.'

Belief in reincarnation has a powerful effect on the way we live in the present. If death is but a new beginning, a bridge across to a new life – and if *how* we live in the present affects who we will be in the next – then it stands to reason that we had better do the best we can now, with this life, in terms of spiritual and psychological development, so that we do not end up the same old person again next time round. This is not always as easy as it sounds.

KARMA AND COMPLEXES

What you are is what you have been, what you will be is what you do now.
Buddha

If you want to know your past life, look into your present condition; if you want to know your future life, look at your present actions.
Padmasambhava

Karma, the law of cause and effect, ensures that we get away with nothing. 'As ye sow, so shall ye reap,' according to the Bible. Gurdjieff said that our being attracts our lives and the trouble is that we do not know ourselves. So, in essence we do not know *how* we are attracting our lives, and therefore we cannot easily change things.

When we do not deal with the causes that bring about unwanted circumstances we make the same mistakes over and over again and fundamentally nothing shifts from within. We may put this down to fate, to life, to the economy. We may blame our parents, our partners, other people. Sometimes we do blame ourselves, but in a negative way, as if there were nothing that could be done about it because we are too stupid, lazy, greedy, etc. Heaping blame on oneself in a negative way, without the accompanying insight and desire to change things fundamentally only creates further negative karmic conditions.

The knowledge that we do not get away with anything should serve as enough of an impetus for us to change our fundamental patterns. But, sadly, this is most often not the case. Will-power can only deal with those things that we already know about ourselves.

Where we seem to be totally powerless is in the area of what Jung called the 'complexes.' These are 'psychic cysts,' accumulations of energy around specific cores.

When a complex is touched by an inner or outer event there is a tremendous reaction, totally out of proportion to the event taking place. The conscious psyche, not knowing where this strong emotion is coming from, cannot deal with it and tries to project it in order to rid itself of it. Of course, this is not done consciously. Projections of complexes are always unconscious.

But how do you know the difference between being angry with someone for a valid reason and a projection? Consider this: a man is driving along the road in an orderly manner when a sports car zooms out of a side street straight into the side of his car. There is considerable damage and the man is furious. He gets out of his car and angrily accuses the other driver of carelessness, stupidity and dangerous driving. He takes his particulars and stomps off, arms raised, head shaking, to take down details from witnesses.

Now compare this with what happened to Graham, a client in his mid-thirties. He sought therapy because he had had a big fright. He was leaving a country hotel in his car and when he came to the end of the long drive that led to the main road he found it blocked by the milkman's van. He sounded his horn angrily, but no one came. He was forced to wait for a few minutes until the milkman returned. But by then Graham could no longer contain his anger. He jumped out of his car, grabbed the milkman by the throat, shook him and threatened to kill him. He stopped just in time for neither of them to get into serious trouble.

The man in the first example was rightly angry and dealt with it appropriately. Graham, on the other hand, was gripped by a complex. When he saw his exit blocked, he did not get angry, instead the anger got hold of *him*. He was totally out of control for a while and saw the whole scenario, momentarily, as a matter of life and death. Then, when his anger had passed, he wondered what had got into him.

Every time we behave irrationally and emotionally, every time we overreact to a situation, become overwhelmed by fear in the face of no 'real' danger, every time we feel something terrible will happen when we are separated from a loved one, we are seized by a complex.

According to Jung a complex is formed as the result of some kind of defeat, maybe death or separation, physical, mental, emotional or sexual abuse, a physical handicap or public shaming and exposure. Whatever the reason, a complex is an essentially *unconscious* component of the psyche. This is because the conscious ego could not deal with the traumatic event and so pushed it into the unconscious. To all appearances it would then seem to have disappeared, but in fact it remains very much alive and, what is more, gathers more and more energy around itself. Complexes can grow into little or huge monsters. They are psychic strategies of survival, but because they are unconscious they are very dangerous. We do not remember where and how they originated and we never know when they are going to surface.

Complexes are like unruly children – they embarrass us when we need to put on a good face, they show us up by their immature behavior, they can be offensive to others and they ruin relationships. Ean and I once invited a well known teacher of philosophy for dinner. She was the author of several books, all dealing with how to live more consciously and how to transform our darker side. All went well to start with. We had prepared a delicious meal and carefully chosen the right wines. We didn't mind when she asked if she could smoke. When she continued to smoke during the meal we were surprised, but *noblesse oblige*, we did not say anything. When Ean offered her some more wine she said, 'No, thank you, I don't need wine.' We let this remark go without comment but she then repeated it, looking me straight in the face, her voice now louder and sharper: 'I don't *need* wine!' I could have reacted sarcastically and made a remark about her inconsiderate smoking or about her lack of knowledge of fine wines and why and how people enjoy them. But I recognized at once that we were in the presence of a complex. Both Ean and I let it pass and she was soon her former self again as if nothing had happened.

People most often do not know that a complex has been aroused and that they are behaving quite irrationally and rudely. What's more, when one is in the grip of a complex it is almost impossible to get out of it. The complex will go underground again of its own accord and the mood will disappear. Our dinner guest most likely associated all people who drink wine with their dinner with alcoholics, and in her past she may well have encountered alcoholism and the abuse that can accompany it. Such a strong reaction would certainly suggest a deep-seated and painful complex associated with drinking.

Rebirthing will make us aware of our complexes, or rather the issues that lie behind them, thus giving us the opportunity to transform them. But it is the process of recognizing, accepting and taking responsibility for them that is the crux of the matter. A severe complex could take three or four sessions or more to work through. It is the Rebirther's responsibility to detect from the initial interview where a person's deepest conflicts and greatest vulnerabilities lie, if at all possible.

THE SOUL

If something indeed survives the death of our physical body, then what is it? A strong light can frequently be seen to be leaving someone's body at the point of death. What is this? Where did it come from and where is it going to? People who work with past-life retrieval believe that this light is the soul, that point of universal love within each and every one of us that is the mediating principle between our existence here on Earth and the realm of divine Spirit.

Some would say that this part of ourselves is not personal, that it belongs to a universal soul and that it is not interested in the individual. But then why is that particular part of the soul inter-ested in inhabiting our particular body? Could it be possible that it may well have been attracted to that body because it would provide the necessary lessons to be acquired during the next lap of its jour-ney? In that case, as the soul wanders from body to body in its quest to draw to itself experiences necessary for its development, it would be reasonable to assume that it also carries the memories of all previous lives. How these then become stored in an individual body-memory system is a mystery. But it could well be that the soul is the carrier of all the memories of all its previous lives in a body.

Another view that I hear expressed from time to time is that what we tune into if we access a past-life memory is not the previ-ous existence of our soul in a body, but remnants from someone else's physical existence, someone who has died but left behind fragments of memory in the atmosphere. I find this notion quite ridiculous and totally without meaning or purpose. When we can create a whole memory system, storing billions of factors, whole libraries even, on pieces of plastic, accessible via the Internet to anyone who can switch on to it, it is quite incomprehensible that personal memories of past lives should be fragments of other people's lives floating about in the air that we tune into.

Could it not be that the soul is both personal *and* universal? Without a personal body, the soul could not express itself in the physical world. And if there were no personal aspect to the soul, then surely all souls would express themselves in exactly the same manner, and all people who have claimed to have made contact with their own souls would rather resemble one another. It is perhaps more reasonable to assume that the soul has a dual consciousness. It is in the body and therefore needs to express itself within and through the limitations of that body, but it is also not of the body, but rather of a higher dimension, the divine and supernatural realms, the blissful fields, whence it seeks to return via its evolutionary journey.

I believe that to become conscious as a soul seeking to express itself through a human being is the goal of human evolution. This soul is not just some concept conveniently employed to describe some vague sense of spirituality. This soul has purpose, power and will. It is the soul that chooses in the first place to incarnate and it is the soul that decides when it is time to leave a body. During its many lives in physical bodies the soul evolves through matter, learning, experiencing and gradually spiritualizing all it touches.

A soul with many lives behind it in which it developed to higher and higher levels of consciousness through a myriad of different kinds of experiences and sacrifices is spoken of as an 'old soul.' A child with an old soul is said to be wise, to have an 'old head on young shoulders.' This is the only reasonable explanation of why some children seem to know so much about human nature, have such sensitive insights and display an altruism that is far beyond their age.

We have no scientific proof that past lives exist, but neither do we have proof that they don't. All we have is our observations and our own and other people's reports of their experience. The same is true of dreams. You know what dreaming is because you do it, and other people do it, too, and they talk and write about their dreams, but no scientist has ever been able to photograph a dream and present us with the hard evidence. With past lives, many people have relived them and they hear and read about other people having similar experiences. In fact, so many people now have past-life flashbacks or meet people who they immediately 'recognize' as someone they have known in another lifetime that we can no longer consider them mere fantasies.

It is sufficient evidence for me that my clients contact past lives regularly without drugs or hypnosis. All they do is breathe in a certain way and the lives, if they are open to them, emerge by themselves, without assistance. You will know, when it happens to you, and you will know that it is not a fantasy. The accompanying vividness, feelings and bodily sensations are too real to be dismissed as a figment of the imagination. Neither can we dismiss them as fragments of collective consciousness that are free-floaters in the sky. The fact is that many people have these experiences just like they have dreams, see a film or look at photograph albums from the past. That these experiences are highly personal and biographical cannot easily be dismissed or discounted. Also, the fact that your life changes very rapidly after you have released and integrated negative past-life memory shows that another stage of the soul's journey has been completed, enabling you to move forward to the next without much hesitation.

But the best proof of all is your own experience. If you are skeptical about reincarnation, don't argue from ignorance or fear, which doesn't make sense anyway. Put your skepticism aside, be adventurous and curious, read up on the subject and talk to people who have already done some personal work on it. In my experience the people who argue most strongly against reincarnation are those who have not studied the subject and those who are most afraid of the unknown.

Reincarnation stands outside religious concepts. Past-life memories are recovered by people from all religions. You do not have to 'believe' in past lives in order to remember one. If you do not think past lives are part and parcel of the totality of our being, if you believe that when you die it is like, as someone put it, 'knocking your head on a door. Bang! That's it and you're gone!', you will probably not bother with past-life therapy at all. If on the other hand you are skeptical but nevertheless would like to explore, then in all likelihood you will find out about the kind of lives you have lived before and what kind of life your soul has chosen for this particular lap of its journey. If you are open to the deeper reaches of your psyche you can contact many past lives, the memory of which can help you understand present difficulties and indeed can give you back qualities and characteristics, such as courage and creativity, that you may have thought were not part of your nature in this life.

If you accept the possibility that this is but one life of many you will most likely have to rethink your whole *Weltanschauung*, your world-view and ideology. You will question the way you live, what you live for, what you value, where you come from, who you are and where you are going. Your attitude to many areas of your life will need to be reviewed in a new light. What is the most important factor in your life and why? How do you spend or not spend your money and why? What use do you make of time? Has your life a purpose, is it meaningful? You will begin to ask these and many other questions relating to how you live it. And by persistently asking you will eventually receive an answer.

8 WORKING WITH PAST LIVES

Our ideas about death have been erroneous; we have looked upon it as the great and ultimate terror, whereas in reality it is the great escape, the entrance into a fuller measure of activity, and the release of the life from the crystallized vehicle and an inadequate form.
Alice Bailey

But in time it shall come forth and be revealed.
Edward Carpenter

In the beginning my Rebirthing clients started to relive past lives spontaneously without any guidance from me. Later, as already explained, when I had come to realize that bodily sensations mostly have a deeper story hidden behind them, I began to encourage my clients to explore these more fully. When bodily symptoms emerged as a result of conscious connected breathing I would ask them to feel them more strongly, get a shape or colour for their pain or emotion or feeling, or simply ask how they got it. I would encourage them to stay with a particular sensation and ask them to allow it to get stronger and stronger. To my amazement, just the thought of doing this could make it happen and then the underlying story would gradually emerge.

In working with past lives you can go back and forwards through various lives and see the patterns, changing from male to female, master to slave or perpetrator to victim. If a past life comes up I encourage the individual to examine that life and see what its essence was. I always try, whenever possible, to take the life to its final stage, to the death scene. The client is encouraged to breathe forward to the last breath or the last heartbeat and surrender him or herself totally to the death experience.

The past-life work I do differs fundamentally from other regression or past-life work because I use the power of conscious connected breathing. Having observed many past-life sessions, I have come to the conclusion that past-life therapy in combination with the breathing work is a powerful therapeutic mix, if not *the* most powerful. At the end of the session, if the breathing was done correctly and for long enough, people feel cleansed and calm, and furthermore, they bring back with them new insights which are of great and spiritual significance and which have life-changing effects.

People often ask how one knows that what one experiences is a past life. Is it not just imagination or a half-remembered historical film or novel? These questions are valid and have interested past-life workers from the beginning. Dr Peter Fenwick, senior lecturer in clinical neuropsychiatry at London University, and his wife Elizabeth have found again and again that people who were hypnotized in order to remember past lives had been influenced, consciously or unconsciously, by the hypnotist. They further found that a great many of these hypnosis-induced past lives had been lived as important personages such as rulers, kings and queens and, therefore, they have dismissed these as not genuine. I would agree with this. How many Mary, Queen of Scots, were there? In Rebirthing, too, some people come up with past lives as Mary

Magdalene or even Christ himself. Many, many people have been convinced that they knew Christ. I think that when these lives come up the individual is tuning into a collective situation. This is still valid, however, in that they are having a powerful experience which, when brought to completion, can bring about healing in the individual as well as the collective.

For me, whether these scenarios are a figment of a person's imagination or not, they are certainly a most marvellous tool for healing deeply seated neuroses, traumas and all manner of physical complaints, and so they are part of my work of cleansing the body-mind so that the life force may flow without hindrance and we may establish, or re-establish, our connection to the larger whole.

DEATH

It is a curious fact that in past-life Rebirthing the only lives to emerge are those that represent unfinished business, and are therefore still causing problems, and that contain at least one traumatic episode. Dr Fenwick found that most people had actually lived boring, ordinary, run of the mill lives. This is what I have also discovered. Many of the lives were uneventful, but what made them important was that a trauma took place which created an energy blockage, either because of the residue of pain or resentment or desire for revenge.

One of the most common past-life traumas to emerge is that of death. In fact, death experiences appear so often and in so many guises that I have come to believe that they are trying to tell us something about our current attitudes towards the subject.

Death is still a great mystery to most of us. A great many people would prefer not to think about it at all. Yet Alice Bailey writes that by the end of the Piscean Age we shall have proof of survival after death. Is the past-life death experience a preparation for dying so that we may lose our fear of it, live life more abundantly and learn to die consciously? Are we in the process of acquiring specific knowledge regarding the human soul? Or is conscious dying becoming necessary in order to avoid souls returning again and again to human bodies and thereby remaining bound to the great wheel of death and rebirth, as the Tibetans believe? Sogyal Rinpoche, the Buddhist meditation master, said with a big chuckle on my husband's TV program about the after-life: 'No good preparing for death when you are dying!' Certainly, it seems worth learning all we can about death while we are still alive. And if we believe that by avoiding making mistakes in this life we will not have to pay for them the next time round, we can live more responsibly than by taking the 'you only live once' attitude, which is marked so often by greed, selfishness, ambition and lack of spiritual values. Even if in the final analysis there truly is nothing after death, we will still have lived a better life by taking responsibility for all our actions.

My own feelings, thoughts and beliefs about death and dying have changed radically since doing Rebirthing. I have witnessed a whole variety of different death experiences and I have seen people blissfully release themselves from bodies that no longer served their purpose. Death, when it comes, is sweet, unless it is sudden or violent, but even then the after-death experience is usually one of light and lightness and warmth and connectedness to a greater whole.

In one past-life Rebirthing experience I had myself, I was a woman who, after nearly being murdered by her Roman soldier husband, went into hiding and spent the rest of her life living in the hills and forests, gathering herbal plants that she used for healing the sick. She eventually died of old age. She lay patiently waiting for death, for she knew it was not far off. Then it came, sweetly, like a warm golden flow, and very gently I felt it move from my feet up through my body and out of the top of my head, taking my soul with it. I knew in that instance that death is a friend and not to be feared.

People who have gone through a past-life death experience in every detail and were able to surrender to the process of separation of soul from body have always lost their fear of death. Their attitude to life has also changed radically, for to consciously experience a death in the smallest detail is a significant experience that leaves its mark on the psyche. Without the fear of death hanging over you, you can live more freely, lovingly and generously. You not only lose your fear of death, but more importantly your fear of life. The same is true of people who have had a near-death experience. In this respect these two types of death experience are identical.

The Tibetan View

According to Tibetans, the thoughts we have at the moment of death are very important, as they condition our next incarnation. That is why learning how to die, learning how to let go of all attachments – including those to one's family and friends and the physical body – in the right way, is of such vital importance. In *The Tibetan Book of Living and Dying*, Sogyal Rinpoche writes about the importance of this final total surrender with great clarity and authority, and I recommend this book highly to anyone interested in the vast knowledge that has been gathered on this subject by Tibetan Buddhists.

Surrendering to death, according to their teaching, is surrender to the transition from one state of being to another. Only by surrendering to and accepting the process of dying can someone who is undergoing a past-life death experience be fully delivered from the karma of that life and perhaps also from that of all lives that went before. The Tibetans teach that each death is an opportunity to surrender and transform so fully that Rebirth becomes unnecessary. It can become, they say, an opportunity for the relinquishing of *all* karma.

A Common Death Theme

A typical pattern that leads to a release through death is easily recognized. A certain time into the breathing cycle I can hear a person's throat becoming constricted and their breathing becomes labored. Suspecting that this is an approaching past-life death, I will let the client breathe for a while longer before I ask what they are experiencing. In most instances they will report tightness in their throat, either due to external or internal pressure. I gently suggest that they might be experiencing a past-life death and that they should allow the symptoms to get stronger.

After some more time has elapsed, during which breathing becomes more and more difficult until it is almost impossible, I suggest that the person 'breathes him or herself forward' to the point of death. From now on I suggest that they take it in slow motion and note the details, whilst continuing to breathe the Rebirthing breath. This way, whatever memory is released from the unconscious body-mind will be 'breathed out' and transformed.

Once a person has 'died' they sometimes literally stop breathing for a short while, as in a breath suspension, or else their breathing becomes very light and barely noticeable. I can tell by the eye move-ments behind their closed lids that they are seeing something on the inside; sometimes they are looking down on their bodies as they are floating above them.

After another interval I encourage a review of the life they are leaving behind and finally a farewell. It is important at this point that the client voices any negative feelings or sadness or anger about that life. Sometimes a catharsis is necessary, sometimes there is silence and sad weeping. Depending on what stage in the breath-ing cycle we have reached, the client then either goes on to another life or moves upward and onward into the light that appears with great regularity after a death.

The variations on the death theme are endless. Dawn, aged thirty, had one isolated breathing session with me when I was on holiday on the island of Majorca, where she was living at the time. She breathed happily for about half an hour and was very much enjoying the freedom it brought. She kept saying how blissful this was, how warm and loving she felt towards her family and, indeed, the whole world. But then things changed and she felt something pressing on her abdomen. I asked her to let that experience get stronger. She was in some kind of room, furniture was turned on its side and the thing pressing down on her was a mahogany chest of drawers. Then, suddenly, she cried out: 'My God, we are on the *Titanic* and we are sinking!'

When Dawn allowed herself to drown consciously and let go whilst she was dying, she was able to step across the threshold from one state of being, one level of consciousness, to another. Her doors of perception widened and she found herself eventually, as happens so frequently, in a sea of bright and blissful light. Finally we reviewed the life she had left behind and several areas of her present life now made more sense to her, particularly the fact that she is afraid of water and is always extremely anxious if her children are anywhere near it.

This took place a couple of years ago, long before it became publicly known that there would be a film about the sinking of the *Titanic*. Dawn recently wrote to me informing me that she had seen the film and that she had a 'very cold, eerie feeling throughout, but especially at the beginning where they inspect the wreck and the word "wardrobe" is mentioned.' She wrote: 'I felt sick and closed my eyes, took a deep breath and carried on.'

Her husband, who has also Rebirthed with me, is afraid of flying. He relived a past life as a pilot who, due to his own negligence, crashed a plane with six other people on board. The insights and the remorse that surfaced during and after this session were of great significance to him.

A different kind of past-life death happened to John, who is in his early forties. In the past life he had spent many years in a dungeon and had slowly gone mad. When I took him forward to the end of his life he started screaming and screaming. Finally he was coughing, spluttering and choking, and sounded as if he was drowning. After he had died we reviewed his life and he told me that 'they,' probably the gaolers, were 'drowning' him by pouring gallons of water down his throat. This was a truly horrible death to watch, but again, when it was over John felt cleansed, released and infinitely lighter. He had a series of awful past-life deaths that always involved violence, torture or injury of some kind. By the time we finished working together he had reorganized his life and had decided to leave England, which was full of bad memories for him, from this life and prior incarnations, and live abroad.

Bad memories were also affecting another client of mine, but unconsciously. She did not want children – and when she finally did get pregnant spontaneously aborted – but went back to a life in which she was pregnant. She was married and was looking forward to the birth, but she and the baby died very painfully during labor. In her current life she kept forming relationships with men who either didn't want children or for one reason or another were unsuitable to start a family with. What she was not aware of in this life was that unconsciously she was afraid of getting pregnant and giving birth, lest she should die again and/or bring harm to the baby. When such a discovery 'clicks,' when deep insight is gained into such a fundamental question as to why one is not committing to a relationship and starting a family, a huge release takes place. It is then possible to psychologically separate this life from a previous one and not repeat the previous life events.

The same can be said of all negative repetitive life patterns. When the unfinished business from a prior life has been released and integrated, a change will inevitably take place. Since our being attracts our lives, our lives will change as our being changes. Another way of putting this would be to say, according to the *I Ching* philosophy, if you change your present, you change your future.

I have come across this unconscious fear of childbirth theme with variations many times. Frequently women who are afraid of becoming pregnant because it ended in tragedy in previous lives marry men who do not want to or cannot father children. One of my clients stayed in a sexless marriage to a homosexual for twenty years and by the time they separated she was too old to bear a child. It was only when she explored her past lives that she discovered that in a previous life she had died in childbirth and then could take full responsibility for being childless.

There are many different types of death and each carries its own story and pathology. Rebirthing can bring them to the surface and cleanse them out of our body-mind system so that they can no longer influence our lives negatively. Often, these past lives and deaths are the root cause of phobias, obsessions and passions. I have come to believe that phobias which usually do not have a rational cause and cannot be traced back to a particular event in this life have their origin in a past life.

PAST LIVES OF QUIET DESPERATION

There is another category of lives that seem to emerge after the more traumatic ones have been released and these are the 'lives of quiet desperation,' lives in which nothing much happened at all and even the death was uneventful. The people who lived them often worked very hard throughout, were very weak or were imprisoned in some way.

I had three such lives emerge in quick succession during one of my own Rebirths. In the first one I was suffering from tuberculosis and lived a very quiet life in the country. I was tired all the time and could not enter into any activity that was the least bit strenuous. In another life I was a retarded young woman in India. Again, the life was very boring; each day was the same as the one before. I lived like this until the day I quietly slipped out of my body. In a third life I was again a young woman, this time in Austria. I wasn't exactly retarded, but I was uneducated, as education was thought to be unnecessary for young ladies; I was naïve and innocent, did not get married and lived a long, uneventful and boring life.

These quiet lives come up with as much regularity as the ones that end with a violent death. On the face of it they seem totally pointless and wasted. But when we examine the learning gained from them we discover that patience, perseverance, humility and ordinariness were their learning and rewards. However, because the boredom and tedium in these lives seem to have gone on forever, they leave a powerful residue: one is terrified of wasting the present life, terrified of 'doing nothing,' achieving nothing and missing valuable opportunities. The result can be a life of activity and hard work, with little opportunity to reflect. But when these past lives are put into perspective, one can allow oneself a little peace and tranquillity.

PAST LIVES AND PRESENT RELATIONSHIPS

Great hates and loves that control, dominate and interfere with our lives can also have their origins in a past life. Relationships that have existed in another lifetime can affect relationships in this life.

We have all heard of love at first sight, for example, and many of us have experienced it not once, but several times. When Elsa first set eyes on John at a funeral she knew that she would marry him. They hadn't even spoken at that point. Within a year of their first meeting, against all the odds, they were indeed married. Furthermore, when I attended the wedding, John told me that when he had first seen Elsa he had said to himself: 'That is the woman I am going to marry.'

Richard, a friend of mine, first spotted his future wife in London's Waterloo station. 'That is the woman I want to marry!' he exclaimed to himself and promptly approached the lady. She was not offended by that bold move; on the contrary, she, too, felt an immediate attraction.

When I first saw my first husband it was from the top of a double-decker bus and I only saw the back of him. He was just entering the house where he lived and where I was also staying. I knew who he was because I had heard his name mentioned the night before. I felt as if I had been struck by lightning and it was clear to me that he would be important to me. When we married a few years later I was also strangely aware that one day we would divorce. Then, when I met my second husband it was an equally powerful love-at-first-sight encounter. I knew in an instant that we would spend many years together, but also that that relationship, too, would not last forever; at the same time, getting married seemed the most natural thing to do. Years later, when my second marriage was going through its final stages of breaking up, I first caught a glimpse across a crowded room of my present husband, Ean, with whom I have now shared many years. Again, I knew that a special relationship would develop, although we only exchanged glances that first time. I didn't even know his name or who he was. We did not meet again until four years later, and still we had to wait and wait until we were both free, inwardly and outwardly, to marry. When we finally did it was at once the most extraordinary and at the same time the most natural thing to happen.

Is it destiny, fate or free will when people have these close encounters that change their lives forever? I believe that it is probably a combination of all three. I believe that when we motivate and activate our inner resources, when we pursue activities for which we have an innate talent, and when this also becomes our work or vocation, we attract the right help, meet the right people and make the right connections.

There is a big difference between doing what you are good at and doing something just for money. I have observed many times over the years that I have worked with people in therapy that when someone finally knows what they really want to do with their life, the strangest synchronicities occur. People appear from all over the place to lend assistance with the task at hand and somehow personal problems are taken care of in the strangest ways. These incidences are of a karmic nature. Other people, whose own lives in some obscure way are invisibly linked with yours, turn up to lend a hand with the next step you need to take because they, too, have a destiny to fulfill, a destiny that happens to touch yours at that point in time.

The right moment in time, the *kairos*, is that point when karma and circumstances conspire to bring what is *ripe* into being. 'When the pupil is ready the Master will appear' the saying runs and the same can be said of personal relationships. When we are *ready*, when preparations are complete, the next stage will arrive, and not before.

For some people this next stage never comes, they are never ready, the moment is never ripe. Their inner response system is shut down. Most people, though, learn and progress through their challenges, pain and suffering, as well as through joy and creativity, and each life crisis is a turning point that contains within it both danger and opportunity. Each crisis, small or large, can lead to a larger vision. Each brings its own challenges and demands for a right response. When a crisis has been successfully addressed, a new set of circumstances and a different chain of cause and effect are created. Successfully and creatively meeting life's challenges often leads to the release of tremendous energy and a renewal of life and its attendant circumstances.

Relationships, like everything else, need to undergo transformation. Nothing can stay the same forever. The purpose of a relationship may be fulfilled at a certain stage and therefore the two people involved may need to go their own way. Many women – and men – who have children with their partners, feel that the purpose of the relationship was to bring those particular children into the world, even if the relationship subsequently 'fails.' With other couples, maybe it is the case that they could work through their difficulties only up to a certain point this time round. In my experience trying to prevent relationship changes from taking place is futile and trying to deny that they are taking place is just as unproductive. Life does not stand still and once subtle relationship changes have begun they will continue.

We know from astrology that under certain planetary transits (the movement of the planets across certain points in the zodiac) existing relationships are likely to break down or at least go through immense difficulties and perhaps temporary separation. Astrologers have also observed that a good solid relationship, made up of two whole people, will become stronger and even more enduring as the result of challenging times that are successfully mastered together.

All relationships, though, only last for a while in any one particular form. All have to go through a period of decay and rebirth in order to survive. Ideally, when a relationship reaches a point of transition, a point when readjustments have to be made by both partners, each will adapt to the new emerging pattern, making whatever sacrifice is necessary and allowing space for something new. To create space for something is to make it holy or sacred. When this need for sacrifice, for letting go of the old in order to make sacred the new, is fully understood by both (or even just the one), a new phase can safely be entered into.

People form new relationships all the time and let go of old ones. There is a time for new beginnings and a time to bring an old phase to an end. This is particularly hard for some people. They want to remain 'friends,' whatever that may mean. What it most often does mean is that one is unwilling, unable or too frightened to let the death of a relationship or a situation occur, leave it behind and move forward. This holding on to past relationships for the sake of friendship not only can hinder the formation of new commitments, but also interfere with one's personal growth. It is often important to be independent and to let others go their own way for the sake of their own individuation. Keeping a relationship afloat for friendship's sake is often nothing more than a continuing desire to exercise control over another. Of course this does not work, and at some level one knows this, but still the holding on continues, sometimes interfering with the lives of more individuals than just the two involved.

Renate and Rudi had been divorced for a few months, but Rudi still came regularly to the house where Renate lived with two of their grown-up children, who resented this very much. It was not that they disliked their father, but they were confused by his inability to create a more independent existence for himself, especially since it had been his adultery that had caused the break-up in the first place. It was only when Rudi recently announced that he is to remarry that everyone could heave a sigh of relief.

I am not suggesting that couples who, for instance, have small children, should, once separated, stop talking to each other – far from it. For the sake of the children it would be better if they could stay together and resolve their difficulties if at all possible, even if it means putting their own desires and ambitions on hold for the time being. If, however, two people can no longer live together because it would be damaging for all concerned, then, although they may be pleasant and friendly to one another, they must start to get on with their own lives as soon as possible.

This is particularly difficult, of course, if one of the partners has been deeply hurt by the other. Many a time I have heard 'I am through with men' or 'I will never trust a woman again' and so on. Worse still is the threat of taking revenge, of violence and of inter-ference with new relationships that the other is in the process of establishing.

If we can look upon relationships as necessary stepping-stones and stages in our evolutionary development when we attract certain individuals, including children, and can recognize when a particu-lar phase has fulfilled itself, we might more readily understand the need to let go and allow ourselves and others the freedom to enter the next phase.

SOUL MATES AND THE RELEASE OF KARMA

Some relationships last until one partner dies, while others are extremely intense, full of passion and adventure, but are gone with the wind within weeks or months. Yet all relationships that we enter into with any kind of commitment, depth and meaning, without exception, have something to teach us. All relationships to a certain extent are *karmic* in that it is our own being, that which we have become over many lifetimes, that attracts our external life.

But there are also those relationships where we speak of two people being 'soul mates.' People describe their soul mate as someone who totally understands them, someone to whom they do not need to explain themselves, someone who seems to know them intimately and who is intensely interested in them. The two often, though not always, share vocational interests and have a strong feeling that they have lived several previous lifetimes together.

Whether or not soul mates exist I do not know, but certainly some people believe they do and 'soul mate' relationships can be extraordinarily fruitful. Yet even the best relationships change with time and can become stumbling blocks if the inevitable difficulties are not addressed and honestly worked through. Change is not a bad thing in itself, of course. It is only when one or both of the individuals involved resists what needs to take place in order for both to grow that the relationship will enter troubled waters or break up.

When people fall passionately in love they often think they have found their soul mate, then when passions cool they realize that they were perhaps a bit hasty in their assumption. On the other hand I have spoken to people whose soul mate was not their lover or husband or wife, but their best mate.

Charlotte's soul mate, for example, is a friend whom she met at university. She is in a long-standing committed relationship with someone else whom she loves dearly, but her relationship with Tom, who is gay, is extremely close in an altogether different way. Although they live in countries far apart, they telephone each other almost daily, spend as much time together as their busy careers allow and tell each other in detail what is happening in their lives. They think nothing of sharing a bed together when necessary, something Charlotte would not do with her own brother. She feels that Tom is a part of herself and that they have known each other through many lifetimes, which would explain the incredible ease that they feel in each other's company.

Hugo and Lisa had also thought that they were soul mates. They had met at university, had been happily married for twelve years and had two delightful children. Lisa felt fulfilled as a wife and mother, was supportive of her husband, a scriptwriter, and had a large circle of friends. Then everything changed dramatically. Hugo was offered an important position in Hollywood, which meant uprooting the family. Lisa was against this from the start. She had no desire to live in California and told Hugo that if he wanted the job that badly he would have to go on his own.

Hugo went through an existential crisis. He loved his wife, children and home, but he also knew that if he wanted to progress as a writer Hollywood could offer him immense possibilities. Finally, after weeks of agonizing, he decided that he would go to Hollywood on his own and try it out for six months but fly home every month for a few days to be with his family. Lisa was most reluctant to agree to this but eventually relented. Within six weeks of his departure from the UK Hugo had fallen in love with one of his co-writers.

When Lisa came to see me she had been separated from Hugo for over two years. This once vibrant woman was depressed; she felt worthless, unwanted and unattractive. What had happened to her and Hugo had hit her with such a force that she had almost completely lost her will to live. She had been so sure that she and Hugo would remain happily married for the rest of their lives it had never occurred to her that he might become attracted to someone else. As a result of her *naïveté* she had not recognized that a new phase was about to enter their marriage, a challenge that could bring with it many opportunities for experience and learning.

During Rebirthing therapy Lisa recognized that after the birth of her children she had totally neglected her own creativity. She had lived her life solely through her husband, her children and her parents. This realization came as a big shock to her, as all big awakenings do. She decided to make radical changes and threw herself into what could be loosely called her own 'self-development.' She started by attending creative writing classes. Pouring out her troubles in early morning writing practice, she found that she actually had a talent for writing, a talent she had previously only recognized and fostered in her husband. As the months went by she wrote more and more and began having articles and short stories accepted by magazines.

As a result of this her relationship with Hugo changed fundamentally. When he came to visit they would discuss her writing achievements and he would help her with assignments and then the outline of her first novel. Although they did not resume their married life, they did become genuinely fond of one another in a totally different way. They talked about what had gone wrong with their marriage and realized that both had been held back by it. Lisa, who had a degree in medieval literature, had stopped reading seriously and had poured her talents into home-making and raising the children. Whilst she had enjoyed being at home and concentrating on supporting her husband and being a mother, she now realized that she had missed the intellectual challenges she had enjoyed before becoming a mother. For Hugo the marriage had indeed become a tender trap. The challenge from Hollywood was what he had secretly dreamed of. Writing for the big screen had always been his ambition and he knew from the start that he would have to accept the offer whether Lisa was behind him or not. He had begun to see the marriage as an obstacle and, he confessed to Lisa later, would have gone to Hollywood even if she had threatened to divorce him.

Whilst at the time the break-up was extremely painful and traumatic for Lisa and the children, looking back, she realized that something needed to change. She hadn't been living her own life.

A year after she started Rebirthing, Lisa had transformed her life. She had made new friends, friends who shared her interests in writing and literature and could inspire and support her in being a woman with individual needs, talents and characteristics. From being a woman who had thought that she was doing the right thing by 'sacrificing' herself for the good of husband and children she had become a creative writer who had found new meaning and joy from within herself. Her writing became the most important activity in her life, a passion that allowed her not only to transform the pain she had previously felt at the break-up of her marriage but also her relationship to her children. With a mother who now had a life of her own, with individual needs to be met, her two daughters also became more self-reliant and free to develop in their own individual ways.

When we examined possible past-life links between Lisa and her husband, she discovered that during several lifetimes she and Hugo had been in relationships where one had been dependent on the other. In one life Lisa was the older sister and Hugo the younger brother. Their parents had died and Lisa had had to take care of Hugo. In another Hugo had been the wife and Lisa a sick husband who needed looking after until his death. In another life they were also married but Hugo (as the husband) had died young, leaving Lisa bereft and heartbroken.

Whatever these past lives are – collective memories, images or previous incarnations – their retrieval and subsequent release from the body-mind memory system brings about healing and peace and a capacity to get on with the next stage of life. Now Lisa's and Hugo's relationship is mended. The karma between them, whatever that might have been, was finished, leaving each free to go their own way. I do not see Lisa any more. She is far too busy now. She writes most days for a few hours, but she has also entered into a new relationship with a man whom she proudly describes as her true soul mate.

DIFFICULT RELATIONSHIPS

For every relationship that ends in greater freedom for both partners, there are many that terminate in hatred, violence and a desire to bring harm to the other person. The deep hurt that two people – be they parent and child, friends or lovers – can inflict on one another can be so wounding that one can remain scarred by it for life.

The damage can be seen when people negotiate divorce settlements. Leila had been negotiating a financial settlement with her husband for several years. Each time she was getting close to reaching an agreement something went wrong and months went by before the proceedings would start again. She wasn't really too bothered about her divorce, although she hoped to get a large sum of money in child support as well as the substantial house. What concerned her more was the fact that there was no new man in her life and that she did not seem to be able to make a success of her acting career.

During a Rebirthing session she hit upon the truth that she was still extremely resentful of her husband for not being a better lover and financial support. She was going to make him pay by holding out for a huge settlement, no matter how long it took. She also realized that at some deeper level she was keeping new relationships at bay as this might jeopardize her negotiations. Rebirthing, though, has a cunning way of cleansing from the body-mind negative thoughts and feelings, and after Leila had expressed her anger for a few minutes, all the while breathing powerfully, she became aware that she really still loved her husband very much, although she could never live with him again. She remembered all the good things they had done together, his support of her when the children were small and his struggle in business to try and keep a roof over their heads. She realized that her resentment at her husband's inability to adequately provide her with a life of riches and luxury was connected to the fact that her father had gambled the family fortunes away, leaving her mother destitute with four young children. Her mother had died at a relatively young age and Leila never forgave her father for what he had done and never saw him again after the family split up. Now she realized that she was still trying to punish her father by wanting to financially ruin her husband.

Subsequent past-life Rebirthing work uncovered several lives of tremendous conflict and strife between Leila and her father, as well as a life in which she had been bitterly betrayed by the man who was now her husband and had almost died as a result of it. However, when we went further back still, Leila discovered a life in which she had been a male member of a primitive warring tribe, mercilessly killing men, women and children in a frenzied attack on another tribe. One of this man's victims had been Leila's present husband, who, a woman in that life, had pleaded for mercy. Without registering any emotion, however, the warrior had slaughtered the whole family. Leila felt deeply shocked and humbled by this experience and it took her a couple of weeks to integrate it. As a result of it she now feels far less inclined to judge others, especially her husband and her father.

When I pointed out to Leila that her life is not likely to take off, that she will have no new relationships and that her work will suffer until she has stopped making impossible financial demands on her husband, instead of trying to justify her actions, she simply nodded and said gently, 'Yes, I can see what you mean.' She decided there and then that she would compromise at the next divorce hearing. It went well and each party got what seemed appropriate. After approximately six years of wrangling, of fighting and of not speaking to one another, the battle was over. Leila emerged wiser, calmer and more balanced. She still does not speak to her husband. She has no interest in him and doesn't like him, for although she did experience a deep love for him in a session, she felt that that love belonged to another 'level,' the love that a soul can have for another. It was on the personality level, the personal small self level, that they could not get on with one another. There are further issues to be explored, but whatever their karma is, whatever has to be worked through this time round, it will have to wait until such time as they can both look at their relationship anew or until another lifetime altogether.

These two examples of karmic relationships may not seem particularly dramatic, but they represent archetypal relationship patterns. For the people involved, the issues of breaking up, and in Leila's case the ensuing divorce and financial settlement proceedings, were experienced as a matter of life and death. It is never the surface story that causes such deep and violent, often self-destructive, emotions to erupt. When the underlying issues are explored, we repeatedly find a story behind the story. It is my belief that unless these earlier stories are transformed, a person will continue to carry unhealthy and unwelcome memories that will perpetuate disturbances in their life.

Rebirthing is a way of removing this pain, allowing the wounds and scars to heal, and letting life flow freely through our veins once more. The old scars often have a physical location around the heart or in the abdomen, where tension has perhaps resided for many years. During Rebirthing these 'energy cysts' can be fully experienced, *prana* can be directed into them and the individual can experience how the power of the breath gently, safely and permanently dissolves them.

LETTING GO

If a karmic relationship is a negative one, it is of immense help to know about the past-life involvements between the couple. If there has been a history of abuse on both sides, the only option open may be to leave the relationship altogether. This in itself can be karmically freeing. The *I Ching* counsels: 'When one cannot love someone, one must not hate them. It is better to have nothing to do with them.'

While on the subject of abuse, it is worth mentioning so-called 'false memory syndrome' and its relationship to past-life therapy. I have worked with people (both men and women) who claimed to have been sexually abused by their father, mother, sibling or other relatives. In the majority of cases this actually did take place. But there are a few instances where what the person reports does not make sense. Their stories are not believed, yet at the same time they are living with a truth that cannot be buried. This is enough to make anyone crazy, and this is precisely how these unfortunate individuals are treated. I am not talking here about cases where an over-eager therapist or psychiatrist has *coerced* someone into believing that they had been abused. The newspapers have been reporting a number of stories of this type lately and the Royal Society of Psychiatrists has this year (1998) issued guidelines warning practitioners not to use any form of treatment whatsoever that might lead to the retrieval of early memories of sexual abuse.

Rape, violence, mutilation and torture are common themes in past-life Rebirthing and someone who was sexually abused in this life often goes straight to a past-life abuse. But people who have not been abused in this life also have experiences of rape and torture. What is much rarer is the situation where someone is convinced that they have been sexually molested by a relative but is in fact remembering a past-life event. I have only come across this particular circumstance three times. Each time, because the past-life event was so vivid, so different from an ordinary memory or fantasy, understanding and healing followed. No organized research has been done, as far as I know, into linking sexual abuse accusations with experiences that actually happened during another incarnation.

For a negative karmic relationship to be healed, both people need to be actively involved in solving the difficulties. Then, when they have made peace, when healing has taken place, when understanding has triumphed over negative emotion, each can go their own way without regret or resentment; when the karma between two people is finished they will part without animosity.

Simply understanding why we are with the people we are with can, however, lead to the mending of many wounds. This can apply equally well to parents and children as to lovers and spouses. Mothers in particular often feel guilty because they prefer one child to another. Some openly admit that they do not like a child, that they wish they had never been born and no matter how much they have tried to accept them the emotional tensions stirred up seem more than they can bear. In such cases, when past-life issues are explored, it is often found that there has been at least one past life, and usually several, in which the pair were involved in an intense relationship.

One mother who felt tyrannized by her young daughter found that in a previous incarnation her daughter had been the wife of her present husband and she had been his sister. They had lived together under the same roof but did not get on and were in competition for the man's affection. In this life the daughter, from a very early age, would come into her parents' bed every night and plant herself between them. The mother was worried that her marriage would break up, as she and her husband were no longer able to share the peace and sanctity of their bedroom without worrying about interruptions and their sex life was suffering badly as a consequence.

After past-life Rebirthing the situation changed dramatically. The mother was able to understand why her daughter was acting in that way and therefore stopped resenting her and suspended her anger and criticism. In this way she stopped perpetuating the old rivalry between the women and with this new approach the whole relationship changed.

An observation made in practically all therapies that deal with the human psyche is that when one member of a family changes, so does every other member. Likewise when one member within a community is healed it has a profound effect on the psyches of all the others. Our being both attracts our life and affects all those with whom we come in contact. When healing of the psyche takes place the authentic Self can emerge, leading us onward to right living, right livelihood and right human relations. Rebirthing facilitates this process, bypassing the *thinking* brain and going instead straight to a blockage in the natural flow of energy.

The process of Rebirthing does not discriminate between events of this life and past incarnations. As always much depends on the practitioner. If the body's signals are read correctly and can be worked with correctly, then there is no reason why a symptom cannot be traced back to earlier origins than this life. The further back we can go into the past, the greater and more extensive will be the healing effect.

Remarkable shifts can take place. The heart centre can open spontaneously and all feelings of separateness can disappear so that the previously despised child, partner or parent becomes a beloved. When the heart is thus opened, hostility and enmity can no longer exist. Forgiveness becomes meaningless, as there is nothing to forgive. I have seen grown men and women weep uncontrollably when the breathing opened their heart and they discovered a profound love for a now dead parent, a love that perhaps did not exist in this life, but in a previous one.

Marina, a painter in her early thirties, wanted Rebirthing because she felt that her marriage to Tom, a psychotherapist, was breaking up. She had convinced herself that he kept falling in love with his female patients. Both Marina and Tom worked from home and they spent nearly all their spare time together, so she really had no rational reason for suspecting him of unfaithfulness, but still she had convinced herself that he would leave, and would do so for another woman. Her fear of losing him was so great that she actually wanted to leave him herself rather than face the pain of him leaving her.

What emerged as the result of a few Rebirthing sessions totally changed Marina's attitude to herself and her marriage. She found that she and Tom had been husband and wife in another life. They were blissfully happy until Tom went away to war and was killed in action. Marina had never recovered from the loss and in the end committed suicide.

Now she had no difficulty making the connection with her fear of losing Tom in this life. Her Rebirthing work had given her a glimpse of her authentic Self, which enabled her to separate the previous life from this. As she grew in confidence she also started taking greater care of herself, became more daring in her artwork, and she and Tom – without her fears standing between them – experienced a Rebirth of their relationship as well.

FATED AND FATEFUL RELATIONSHIPS

When we become very deeply and emotionally involved with another person they become our fate. For better or worse we will need to see the relationship through to its end. In such a relationship there will be something to be learned from the other person and a debt of some kind to be repaid.

This repayment, for good or ill, can take various shapes or forms. What generally happens in a relationship of this kind is that one person becomes the container whilst the other the contained. The container, as the word suggests, contains or holds the relationship, ensuring that it has a space in which to develop and a future to develop towards. If the other has an addiction problem, for instance, the container will try and help. Or, if the other feels insecure about commitment and repeatedly breaks off the relationship and always returns, the container provides a kind of safe haven for the contained until, it is hoped, the contained becomes more mature, calms down and is able to commit. In most situations like this, if a change does not occur in the behavior pattern of the contained, the relationship finally breaks up and both will most likely go on to find a similar situation.

In some cases, however, the relationship continues through hell and high water, with both partners finding themselves committed to acting out a dramatic play that may or may not have a happy ending. In such a scenario, two people who often seem to be totally unlike one another, who fight a great deal and do not even seem to like, let alone love each other, will remain together regardless. Why is this? Why do they do it?

Projection

One of the reasons why such relationships continue is that each person is living out a 'shadow' part of the other. By 'shadow' I mean the part of ourselves that contains everything that we consider unacceptable in ourselves, everything that we have not yet made conscious and all the vast potential that is still awaiting development, as well as that inner life that is as yet unlived.

When we meet another person who seems to have some or many of the qualities that also belong to us but that we are not aware of in ourselves, a 'projection' takes place. As explained earlier, the word 'project' comes from the Latin *projicio ject*, which means to throw forth. When we meet another person in whom we unconsciously recognize a part of ourselves, we throw forth – project onto – the other our very own talents, abilities and power, as well as our more negative traits such as stupidity, cruelty, awkwardness, etc. Because these have been resting deep within our psyches, we experience them as coming from the other person, not as part of ourselves at all.

If you find this hard to believe, just think about all those couples who fall in love and look upon the beloved as the most wonderful being in the world. The pair pledge eternal love and might even become engaged or married. But when the 'being-in-love' stage – that 'divine madness' – cools, little remains of that initial fiery passion. The other has become an ordinary mortal with all kinds of human faults. Then the couple may either split up or move on to the next stage and begin the business of adjusting to one another, working through their difficulties, learning to grow through relating and facing the enormous challenges that need to be met in any relationship if it is to last. Relationships do present us with by far the most difficult challenges.

We would probably all be more inclined and willing to co-operate with others, individually or in groups, in order to establish right relationships, if we were more conscious of our dark side and therefore did not project characteristics onto others that properly belong to ourselves. What also happens when we thus project is that we throw out (even throw away) a part of ourselves that is necessary for us to become the person we are meant to be.

Fay, for example, is a gentle, loving and very kind mother and wife. She is adored by her family and many friends. She is always prepared to be there for anyone who needs help and assistance. There is only one problem in her life and that is her husband Jim, who is an alcoholic. Each night he comes home with a bottle of whisky, pours himself a treble and starts cooking. This in itself does not perhaps sound too bad. But by the time dinner is ready Jim will have downed half a bottle. By the time they are halfway through their meal he will be lecturing and preaching, shouting and at the same time crying and professing his love to all. His children try and avoid him and do not bring their friends home any more.

Fay and Jim stopped going out as a couple a long time ago. Fay would never know whether Jim would pick an argument with someone or sentimentally start crying and tell total strangers he loved them. They still entertain at home from time to time, but even when Jim is being amiable, the evenings nearly always end in vicious arguments with their guests. Yet, on the occasions that I have witnessed them, these are not provoked by Jim but by Fay. On close observation, when she herself has had a few too many, she starts to criticize not only Jim but also her guests. She creates this disharmony in such a subtle way that unless one is skilled in this type of observation no blame could possibly be attached to her. So Jim, although he needs to take responsibility for his own bad behavior, has become a carrier for her darker side. All her difficulties can be blamed on his drinking problems.

These two people will stay together until one of them dies. Fay needs Jim to carry her angry and bitchy side, and the side that is not in control of her life, and Jim needs Fay to take care of him, to be there for him and keep the home and some sense of normality intact. He needs Fay as his container. This pattern of relationship is more common than it would seem.

Taking Back a Projection

We all project onto others – that is the gift of relationship. It is through this projection that we become aware of who we are. In the other, you can admire or hate that side of you that is shown to you as a reflection. Other people are the mirrors for our unknown selves. However, not everything we see in another person is a projection. We may simply detect a characteristic in someone and either like it or not. Normal evaluation of a person or a situation is not a projection! It is only when our reaction to the other is accompanied by a *strong emotional charge* that we are in the presence of a projection. When you become irrationally upset because of what someone says to you, or you fall head over heels in love, or are enraptured with someone for whatever reason, you can be pretty sure that you are projecting, throwing forth, onto the other, a part of yourself.

To recognize projections and to take them back is an important aspect of psychotherapy. It means taking responsibility for ourselves and the end of blaming our woes on others. It also means, just as importantly, owning our more positive qualities that up until now we have only been able to admire in others.

Rebirthing provides a tremendous opportunity for such a process. When an altered state of consciousness has been reached through conscious connected breathing, one's relationships to others often become crystal clear. Parents realize how deeply they love a child they have been having great difficulty with, have been too harsh with and have resented. A woman will suddenly become aware that her lover reminds her of her cruel father and that she has been projecting her fears onto him. When she realizes that she has been trying to resolve with her lover issues which properly belong to her relationship with her father, there is frequently an immediate improvement.

Antonia was deeply in love with Kirk. She admired his professional success, his talents and his worldly standing. She only saw him at weekends, though, because he was always too busy to see her during the week. She accepted this because she hoped that eventually he would return her love and would want to marry her. But the years went by, the situation did not improve and although she broke off the relationship several times she continued to love and admire him and felt that they definitely had a future together. All this time her own life was on hold. She had no energy to develop her own brilliant career, although she desperately wanted one. Then, after eight years of such 'togetherness,' Kirk fell in love with someone else, leaving Antonia totally devastated and heartbroken.

During her first Rebirthing session it came to light that Antonia could not let go of projecting her own brilliance and cleverness. Kirk had become the carrier of her intellect and power, the only person in the world she could ever love, admire and adore. Projections of this kind make us blind to reality. Kirk had given Antonia no indication whatsoever that he would settle down with her, yet she had continued year after year deluding herself that one day he would do just that.

As we probed her past more deeply a whole series of previous lives were uncovered in which Antonia had 'served' others. She had a strong sense of not having the right to live her own life. What surprised her most of all was that she was actually waiting for someone to rescue her, to bring her on a platter that wonderful life that she had been dreaming of for years. Her self-worth was extremely low, yet she was acutely aware of her own intelligence, even arrogantly so. But her past-life pattern prevented her from developing her own powers and creating her life in such a way that she no longer needed to rely on others for it.

We 'breathed' through several of the lives in which Antonia had been poor, imprisoned, ill or in some other way not able to live the life she desired and slowly changes could be seen in her. She became more ambitious, more disciplined in her own working life and stopped expecting her salvation to come through a relationship. The Rebirthing sessions were occasionally supported by an hour of only talking, but the leaps and breakthroughs came during those moments of altered states of consciousness when Antonia could see the pattern of her various incarnations and its significance.

I have found that when someone is in love with another and is dazzled by them, but the other person does not feel the same and behaves selfishly, without consideration and takes the relationship for granted, there is no cure for it. One needs to wait until the projections have been withdrawn, or until one falls in love with someone else and transfers the projections onto that person, or until the other behaves in such an appalling manner that one has no choice but to leave.

Rebirthing can be of great assistance in helping one to see one's projections, owning them, taking responsibility for them and transforming them into creative energy, thus opening up new pathways to the future. It can also help with the development of trust, something that can become very damaged through relationships. During a typical Rebirthing session there comes a moment when absolutely all is well, when you feel totally at one with yourself and the world. All problems have disappeared, all conflicts have ceased, all tensions on all levels have gone. It is in these moments that we are able to gain a glimpse of the essential harmony that exists in the universe. A deep cleansing has taken place on an inner level and all negative thoughts and feelings have been removed, leaving us feeling not only 'filled with light and love,' as many people have described it, but also completely trusting that 'all manner of things shall be well' and that the right things will happen from now on.

Most people who seek therapy of one kind or another have never experienced this deep and total trust in a carrier of the life force. For those who are afraid of reliving and releasing past-life memory, who fear life-changing revelations about themselves and others, who fear a confrontation with their dark side and who do not trust that deep within themselves there dwells a guiding light that ensures that 'all shall be well,' may the following poem serve as an inspiration and reassurance. It was written by the poet Victoria Mosley, who came to me for ten Rebirthing sessions in a week. Her life at that time was chaotic and uncertain and she had reached that unmistakable and crucial juncture that creative people frequently experience before a major breakthrough in their work.

Victoria worked very deeply, contacting within herself lives and experiences that were at times almost unbearably painful, but which, as she said, gave her 'a direct experience of the numinous, a profound sense of peace and unity with the cosmos, and understanding of death and reincarnation.'

ALTERNATING LIVES

Shadows from the dawn of time
fragments of the lives I've left behind,
I breathe the breath that brings dreams back to me,
coursing through my bones with painful ecstasy.

The blind man robbed of sight
to heal his tribe,
the priestess robed in gold
dragged from her holy office
by marauding nomads,
I feel the sadness of unfinished lines
seeing from her eyes the star struck sky
above my head five thousand years gone by;

the breathing drags me deeper
into the flower's kernel,
a young babe's cry,
the universe laid out in pulsing waves
of living sea,
connecting everything to you and me.

High in my body like a radiant grid
I hum meridian blue,
my mind floats in God's ocean
looks down with calm emotion
at this creature I believe was me.

In the space outside the moment
in this time which curves with blue flecked motion
like an arched rainbow of belonging
I lie in sensuous overstatement,
knowing and not knowing,
being, intimately revealing,
feeling I can't prolong these instants,
plucked like the feather of a bird of paradise
from the kaleidoscope of heaven

to rest with me.

9 TOWARDS THE LIGHT

But always there is a persistent over-shadowing light, from which a stream of light pours down into the phenomenal man.
Alice Bailey

The balancing of opposite qualities in the field of emotions and sentiments needs the help of a superior regulating principle of a mental and spiritual nature.
Roberto Assagioli

Light, colour and significance do not exist in isolation.
Aldous Huxley

The light I perceive is not of a local kind, but much brighter than the cloud which supports the sun... What I see or learn in such a vision stays long in my memory. I see, hear and know in the same moment... While I am enjoying the spectacle of this light, all sadness and sorrow vanish from my memory.
Hildegard von Bingen, *Acta S. Hildegardis*, Vol. 197, col. 18

The vision of a light that is brighter than bright yet does not hurt your eyes is a common experience of many mystics. Jung discusses the phenomenon in the foreword to *The Secret of the Golden Flower*, quoting from the writings of Edward Maitland. Through deep contemplation Maitland was able to traverse successive spheres of different dimensions, an experience he compared to being a part of the universe as well as being aware of his own inner system. By an immense effort of will and intense concentration he focused all his energy on the idea of unity and suddenly found himself confronted with 'a glory of unspeakable whiteness and brightness, and of a lustre so intense as well-nigh to beat me back.' Not content with this, he wanted to pierce this 'almost blinding lustre' to see what lay behind it and with a final tremendous effort managed to break through to the centre of this light. There he saw what he calls 'the double aspect of God' – God as a form and God as a force, 'Love as well as Will, the Feminine as well as the Masculine, Mother as well as Father.' Then he stopped breathing. He was not holding his breath; his breathing had simply stopped. He felt as if someone else was doing the breathing inside him. He interpreted his inner breather as the 'inner Christ' of the apostle Paul, the 'spiritual and substantial individuality ... representing, therefore, the *rebirth* of man on a plane transcending the material' [my italics].

When I read this I was tremendously excited. Here, in the foreword to a book about Chinese yogic philosophy was a description of an experience that I have had many times during my Rebirthing sessions and one that many of my clients have also had. When someone sees and then enters the bright light, they undergo a transformation of the greatest significance, even if they do not always understand their experience. Sometimes they encounter Christ or God, while at other times it is a wise being, perhaps someone familiar, who has 'always' been with them. I encounter the Buddha quite regularly myself. The reverence I feel is indescribable. And always this experience is accompanied by a deep insight that is needed at that particular time.

The first time I experienced the light I was breathing with about twenty other people. For a while I had been watching inner universes unfold, full of stars and nebulae, when a small extremely bright light appeared. It grew brighter and bigger and came closer and closer until it was touching me. At this point I felt myself drawn upward into the centre of it. I felt surrounded by unconditional love, tremendous warmth, compassion and a total sense of belonging and one-ness. At the same time I was also aware of an immense overwhelming force. It literally took my breath away. I *knew* that what I was looking at was the face of God. How, I don't know. It was simply a fact that I knew. What I saw that day has stayed with me ever since but it is impossible to describe that numinosity, that supernatural vision, to anyone who has not had a similar experience.

The Secret of the Golden Flower, in which Jung quotes Maitland's experience, is a practical esoteric guide to the attainment of higher consciousness. Originally the teaching was only transmitted orally until it finally appeared in print in the eighteenth century. The Golden Flower is the Light of pure consciousness, the pure everlasting energy of the great Creator. The guarding of this Light within is said to prolong life. The book talks of the need to make the Light circulate within. It is this that is the great secret of the Golden Flower. If one can systematically make the Light circulate, which takes a whole 'fire-period' (probably one year), then the spirit-body is created. In order to attain this state one needs to apply clarity and intelligence and be in a tranquil and meditative state of mind, otherwise the Light cannot stay and nothing will be achieved. In this attitude of deep contemplation, with the mind stilled, the inner centre, the heavenly heart, will spontaneously manifest. If no obstacle remains, on a mental, physical or emotional level, the pure spiritual centre can be reached.

In *A Treatise on White Magic* Alice Bailey reminds the esoteric student of the necessity to 'hold his mind steady in the light' and says that when he can do this 'he will achieve power and possess the single eye which will rebound to the glory of the indwelling divinity.' But the student must work to master this process by manifesting some greater purpose in life so that the incoming power may be used selflessly for the good of others. Personal desires must be transmuted into real and vital aspiration. This, Bailey says, is the meaning of light.

In Rebirthing experiencing the light is always of great significance and presages the possibility of a transformation of consciousness and spiritual emergence. If after a light experience an individual continues to practice conscious connected breathing, meditates and concerns themselves with the 'stuff of the soul,' they will have begun the construction of the light-body.

THE BREATH SUSPENSION

There comes a point during a Rebirthing session when, if the breathing is strong and continuous and if the individual is able to open sufficiently to the incoming energies, they will stop breathing. In my view, this 'breath suspension' is the secret of successful Rebirthing.

It is also one of the strangest phenomena I have ever witnessed or experienced. Breath suspension is not the same as holding your breath. Firstly it happens quite naturally and without conscious intention, and secondly there is no effort involved, as there is in holding the breath. It frequently happens during a breathing cycle, perhaps three or four times. Most people fall unconscious just prior to it, but in some cases the person is acutely aware of what is happening. At this point the whole body begins to breathe inwardly, or, as Maitland felt, the 'inner Christ' breathes. The 'breath within the breath,' through which enlightenment is achieved, is also mentioned by the fifteenth-century mystic poet Kabir. This statement is not just poetical language but a description of an actual experience.

I have never known anyone come to harm as a result of a breath suspension or this altered state of consciousness. Breathing will start again quite naturally by itself. But why does it happen at all? I could understand that it might occur when one breathes very fast and hyperventilates, but quite often a person is breathing gently, rhythmically and effortlessly and will still suspend the breath.

I once asked Stan Grof, who developed a breathing therapy called 'Holotropic Breathing,' where he thought people went during a breath suspension. 'They go into the void,' he replied. Edward Maitland thought that when you go into deep contemplation, you eventually make contact with the source of the original idea, the divine spirit. Is it possible that we can breathe ourselves to this divine source or spirit? Could the breath suspension perhaps be a space of transition, during which a profound shift in consciousness can take place. Do we, during these few minutes of apparent unconsciousness, pass through a gateway that our waking consciousness would fear and resist and thus hinder or prevent altogether? 'The mind is the greatest slayer of the truth,' says Madame Blavatsky in *The Secret Doctrine*. Would our minds, with their incessant need 'to know,' prevent this shift to another dimension? Or is the quality of the conscious mind such that it is incapable of making the transition from one realm of consciousness to another?

Jill Purce, who works with the healing power of the voice, talks about the 'magic garden' that you go to at the end of the exhale. You can reach this garden if you keep exhaling. Even when no exhale remains you keep on exhaling, thereby suspending your breath, until you find yourself in this magical realm.

DARKNESS AND LIGHT

On occasions when I have Rebirthed myself and paid complete attention to strong full circular breathing, the entering into the light has always been preceded by the blackest darkness. Each time I was afraid that I was about to die, but each time I could hold onto just enough consciousness to know that I was undergoing a profound experience, that I had entered another world. Thus I was able to push myself just that little bit further and break through into the light.

Hildegard von Bingen also talks of a darkness that is at its blackest when 'the heavenly heart suddenly begins a movement. This is the return of the light, the time when the child comes to life.' Other mystics, too, have borne witness to the blackest darkness that gives birth to light. If light is indeed born out of darkness then it would appear impossible to enter it without also first entering the darkness. But what the true significance of this is we do not know.

THE BLISSFUL FIELDS

Another phenomenon that occurs with great regularity when I give myself a session is that I feel a ring of energy surrounding and going right through my body, starting at my feet. Gradually this energy will move upward through my body. I can only describe it as a powerful electrical charge. When it reaches my head I sometimes lose consciousness and when I come round I am in the light, the 'blissful fields,' completely at peace with myself. All conflict has gone and my body and mind feel totally at one, light and floating. My limbs feel light and all joints totally cleansed. At other times I remain conscious and am able to look into the eye of spirit itself. At this point it is vital that consciousness is held steady in the light so that the blissful fields can be entered with full awareness. The bliss and peace I and many of my clients experience is always accompanied by this heightened awareness, an illumination of the mind, that casts light on areas of the psyche that normally remain hidden.

The following example will illustrate how such an experience can effect someone's life. During her first Rebirthing session, Eleanor, an attractive powerful businesswoman in her late forties, retrieved a long-forgotten memory. Her breathing session went through various stages, ending with entering into the light.

The memory then erupted suddenly and with such tremendous clarity that it transformed her totally. During this session she kept thinking about one of her female employees. She had no idea why this should be of any significance. She then realized that she was treating this young woman like a daughter. Staying with this thought, she broke into sobs and cried for a long time. She had suddenly 'remembered' that she had desperately wanted a daughter but had given birth to only boys, four of them. It is necessary to point out here that this had not been in her consciousness at the time of the session or at any other time previously. She gets on well with her sons and always thought that she preferred boys. But she was now aware that deep inside she felt cheated by not having a daughter.

I did not see Eleanor again for at least two years as she lives thousands of miles away. But during that time she entered therapy and got to know herself better. When we met again she was a changed woman – softer, gentler and infinitely happier. Her values had changed, too. She now arranges her life so that she has more time to do the things she enjoys. She told me that she needed all of those two years to 'recover' from her breathing experience and from the lie she had been living, but that she would never turn the clock back and be her former self again. This transformation may appear insignificant in the large scheme of things, but for Eleanor it made all the difference between living her life unconsciously and awakening to the fact that there is another dimension to be lived, an authentic Self that most people cannot even dream of.

OCEANIC BLISS

One of the reasons Rebirthing speeds up our personal development is that it facilitates contact with the Higher Self. How does it do this? In the same way that it facilitates contact with negative and harmful memory. If we remember that on the incoming breath we bring into our bodies huge amounts of *prana*, of life force and spiritual energy, we will understand that not only does the breath act as a provider of oxygen but also as our prime contact to the source of divine power.

Harish Johari writes in *Leela*:

Prana is élan vital, *the life force itself. In Sanskrit it is synonymous with life, and is also the name of the life-breath we take in with each inhalation... From birth to death* prana *plays a crucial role in our lives.* Prana is *life.*

In the *Bhagavad Gita*, Krishna elaborates on this principle by telling Arjuna:

For I am Brahman
Within this Body
Life immortal
That shall not perish:
I am the Truth
And the Joy forever.

Brahman is the all-pervading life force, the ultimate Unity. The *Bhagavad Gita* states that essentially all there is comes from Brahman and all will return to Him. We meet with this concept of divinity also in Christianity and other religions. However, the *Gita* stresses that essentially man is also God, that God resides in man and that this has always been so and will always remain so: 'There was never a time when I did not exist, nor you... Nor is there any future in which we shall cease to be.' It teaches that union with the divine is possible in *this* lifetime, not only after death, and that this can be achieved after long periods of study, meditation and right living.

When I had my first experience of merging with the divine light, an experience that was of overwhelming intensity, heat, brightness, beauty and love, I *knew* that I was in the presence of something far greater than myself, unimaginably powerful yet immensely kind and all-embracing. And it came from within myself! I had penetrated to an inner core of extraordinary spiritual power that was connecting me to a far greater transformative force. Later, upon reflection, I realized that the two powers, the inner and the outer, are essentially one and the same.

The ultimate purpose for me in my work as a Rebirther, therefore, is to make contact with this divine power that dwells deep within each and every one of us. When all that stands in the way of the natural flow of life and light has been released from our body-mind system, the way to contacting the higher or transpersonal realms of spirituality and the numinous opens. Like me, those who have had this direct contact know it and will never forget it, and will never be the same again.

When the way of ascent has become clear, people first report intense inner visions. Normally, when we close our eyes, we see nothing, or at least we think we see nothing. We might see a few shades of light and dark, depending on the light outside, but basically, when we turn our eyes inward, we see nothing much. During a Rebirthing session, however, after a certain time of breathing, the inner vision becomes clearer. A common experience at this point is the glimpsing of an inner universe. To start with only simple patterns of grey and dim light appear. But gradually vivid, fluorescent and other-worldly colors can be seen. These colors are so special, so unusual, so bright, so vivid and so pure and clear, that all one can do is marvel with great awe at this inner unfoldment of dramatic shape-shifting and colour.

At this point one becomes acutely aware of a magical world. We can now contact this world because we have transcended the dullness, density and ordinariness of our physical bodies. When we allow ourselves to open, to let go and to cross the threshold between here and there, between the world of the ego and the inner world of the Self, without drugs and without hypnosis, the Otherworld of sheer splendor and opulent ostentation becomes as real as our everyday existence. We know it exists because, while totally lucid, we can see it as clearly and vividly (perhaps even more so) as anything in ordinary life. And as only the special breathing technique has been used, there are no after-effects from drugs, only a tremendous sense of amazement and privilege at having been allowed a view of these higher reaches of human nature.

But it is not only the inner seeing that brings about a rapid alteration in consciousness, but the total merging with this oceanic experience. When we step outside our normal sensory awareness, when we allow ourselves to shift across into the Otherworld and become one with it, we can begin to know something of the visions and experiences of the saints and mystics.

Huxley speculated that humans will always need to avail themselves of some kind of drug in order to effect the transition from ordinary consciousness to the Otherworld. Perhaps the experiences induced by mescaline are more powerful – after all, during these hallucinogenic episodes the outer world also appears as transformed – but I have yet to be convinced that some of the Rebirthing experiences that I and many others have met with are not as vivid, significant, life-transforming and extraordinarily beautiful and spiritual, and with the added bonus of being health-enhancing.

Just as mescaline will not necessarily induce a supernatural vision, so Rebirthing can also lead a person into a dark, frightening and hostile realm, where only danger seems to await. But only on very rare occasions, when standing before the portals of the dark, forbidding regions of the psyche, has someone refused to go any further. This reluctance needs to be respected. Not everything can be experienced at once. But when a willingness to go on is present, despite the great fear that might also be there, the opportunity arises to dissolve all grasping, all ambition and all need to control one's own life. *Then* there is the possibility, as Traherne says, to 'let the sea flow in our veins ... and let the stars be our jewels.'

It would appear to those who have gone down this road that this direct perception of the Otherworld, of dark and light, of strange lands and beings, of supernatural colors, feelings and sensations, is necessary to make sense of the world as it truly is.

Without such direct contact is it possible to remain sane is the big question that Huxley posed.

Perhaps the fact that access to this divine light (and perhaps divine life) has now become much more readily available in a way that had not existed before, through Rebirthing and various types of meditation for instance, and without too much effort, indicates that humanity as a whole is ready to speed up the evolution of consciousness. It might also indicate that more people than ever before are now sufficiently developed mentally to contain this light and that our personalities are strong enough to be carriers for these heightened vibrations.

There is a strong case to be made for taking the slow, more passive path of psycho-spiritual development and for many people that is probably the only right way. There is a place for analytical (talking) psychotherapy. It is a much slower way, but one that is of immense value to many people. People like to talk, they like to tell their story and they like to feel relatively safe when doing soul-work. Rebirthing is generally not chosen as a way forward by the faint-hearted or by those who are terrified of 'loss of control' or by those people who essentially do not wish their lives to change. Rebirthing confronts one repeatedly with 'not knowing,' with situations in which there is no certainty of what the outcome might be. It is a powerful lesson in learning to 'trust the process,' in acquiring confidence that there is a part inside us that is totally well and healthy, that can connect to a power far greater than anything imaginable, and that can lead us through and out of darkness into light.

An immediate psychic experience of divine light – 'fiery light with lightning flashes,' as Hildegard von Bingen put it – will speed up a person's development by providing the life force that feeds the spirit- or breath-body. It will heal inner wounds and our alienation from ourselves and others and, above all, build a bridge between self and the highest unity, pure cosmic essence, the universal mind. Rebirthing, practiced correctly, is a fast and safe route to igniting the inner spirit with the universal spirit that enters our bodies on the incoming breath. That incoming spirit is the essential life force that is the very stuff of consciousness.

Jung tells us that the spirit is a guiding principle of life that strives towards superhuman, shining heights, while in Chinese yogic philosophy the goal of dedicated and protracted spiritual practice is the obtaining of the breath-body, which is immortal. There are many systems that offer courses in spiritual development which may or may not include special diets, meditation, yoga and movement. Rebirthing offers another dimension and is complementary to all of the above.

You do not need to have a degree in meditation, philosophy or psychology or have practiced yoga for many years to enter a breath-induced mystical experience. What you *do* need to bring to a session is a willingness to allow whatever the breath brings up to emerge into consciousness. You will also need to lay aside any cynicism you may hold concerning so-called 'New Age' methods of therapy. If you have a history of mental, emotional or physical abuse you will also need to suspend your lack of trust in others for at least the length of the session in order to work with the therapist. Suspicious, negative and skeptical thinking could get in the way of a breakthrough experience and a spiritual emergence. If the mind is very strong it is possible to hold onto established thinking and beliefs in order not to alter one's views about a negative world. However, some people (and I was one of them) enter Rebirthing therapy with no hope of significant changes taking place, yet the breathing is powerful enough and alters their consciousness sufficiently to bypass any old views and ideas that are not conducive to spiritual development and emergence.

To be understood the oceanic experience needs to be experienced. The healing powers, deep significance, inspiration, supernatural beauty and holiness that can be contacted are part of human reality, a reality infinitely subtle, benevolent and sacred. This Otherworld is a world that exists right here and now, it is not illusory or merely imagined, to some it is a fact of life.

For those who *know*, what I am describing here is familiar, but for those who have not yet had an experience of entering that other dimension all this will have little meaning. I do hope, however, to have aroused sufficient curiosity for you to experiment, if possible, with a skilled Rebirther who has him or herself visited transpersonal realms.

SELECTED BIBLIOGRAPHY

Bailey, Alice A., *A Treatise on White Magic*, Lucis Press, 1980
--, *A Treatise on the Seven Rays*, Vols I (1971), II (1974), III (1975), Lucis Press
--, *The Externalisation of the Hierarchy*, Lucis Press, 1981
--, *Death: The Great Adventure*, Lucis Press, 1985
Carus, C. G., *Psyche: On the Development of the Soul*, Spring Publications, Inc., 1989
Chopra, Deepak, *Quantum Healing*, Bantam Books, 1989
Grof, Stanislav, *Beyond the Brain*, State University of New York Press, 1985
Huxley, Aldous, *The Doors of Perception* and *Heaven and Hell*, Flamingo, 1994
Ingerman, Sandra, *Soul Retrieval*, HarperSanFrancisco, 1991
Johari, Harish, *Leela*, Routledge & Kegan Paul, 1980
Jung, C. G., *The Collected Works*, Vol. II, Routledge & Kegan Paul, 1973
Kaptchuk, Ted J., *Chinese Medicine*, Rider Books
Maciocia, Giovanni, *The Practice of Chinese Medicine*, Churchill Livingstone, 1994

Minett, Gunnel, *Breath & Spirit*, The Aquarian Press, 1994

Mosley, Victoria, *Passing Through*, Odyssee Press, 1998

Onians, R. B., *The Origins of European Thought*, Cambridge University Press, 1951

Swami Pramhavananda and Christopher Isherwood (trans.), *Bhagavad Gita*, Vedanta Press, 1987

Yogi Ramacharaka, *Science of Breath*, L. N. Fowler & Co. Ltd, 1960

--, *Hatha Yoga*, L. N. Fowler & Co. Ltd, 1981

--, *Yogi Philosophy*, L. N. Fowler & Co. Ltd, 1983

Rinpoche, Sogyal, *The Tibetan Book of Living and Dying*, Rider Books, 1992

Rumi, Jalal al-Din, *Daylight*, trans. Camille and Kabir Helminski, Threshold Books, 1994

Thich Nhat Hanh, *Our Appointment with Life*, Prallax Press, 1990

Trungpa, Chogyam, *Shambhala: Path of the Warrior*, Shambhala, 1995

Upledger, John E., *Your Inner Physician and You*, North Atlantic Books, 1991

Wilhelm, Richard (trans.), *The Secret of the Golden Flower*, Routledge & Kegan Paul, 1931

Woolger, Roger J., *Other Lives, Other Selves*, Crucible, 1990

TRAINING

TRAINING IN REBIRTHING THERAPY

For a list of IBF recognized Rebirther training schools contact:
The International Breath Foundation
101 rue de Bosnie
1060 Brussels
Belgium
Tel: +322 5373395
Fax: +322 5375831

Deike Begg trained with:
Diana Roberts School of Rebirthing
Diana@dianaroberts.co.uk.

TRAINING IN PSYCHOSYNTHESIS

The Psychosynthesis and Education Trust
92–94 Tooley Street
London SE1 2TH
UK
Tel: (+)171 403 2100
Fax: (+)171 403 5562

Revision
97 Brondesbury Road
London NW6 6RY
UK
Tel: +(0)181 357 8881

Association for the Advancement of Psychosynthesis
PO Box 597
Amherst
Ma. 01004
USA
Tel: 413 253 6971

TRAINING IN PAST-LIFE THERAPY

Woolger Training Seminars
51 Elting Avenue, New Paltz
NY 12561
USA
Tel: 845 255 0516
rogerwoolger@earthlink.net
and
Briarwood
Long Wittenham
Oxon.
OX14 4QW
UK
Tel/Fax: + (0)1865 407996
Woolger.uk@talk21.com

INDEX